P

INVESTIGATORS

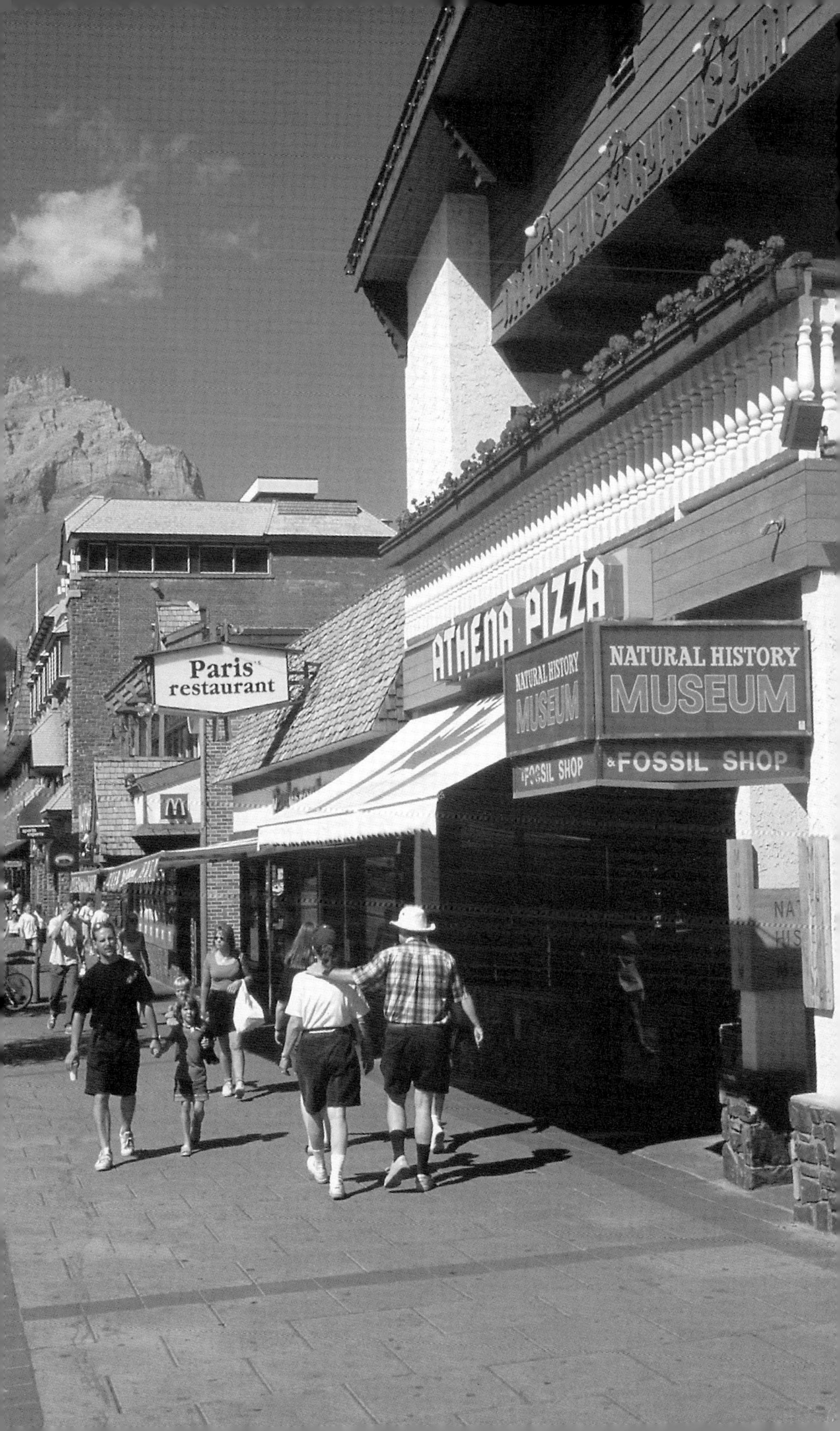
Paris
restaurant
ATHENA PIZZA
NATURAL HISTORY
MUSEUM
&FOSSIL SHOP
NATURAL HISTORY
MUSEUM
FOSSIL SHOP

PRIVATE
INVESTIGATORS

Undercover in Public Space

Essays by Kathryn Walter

and Kyo Maclear

WPG Editions

BANFF CENTRE PRESS

Private Investigators: Undercover in Public Space

Canadian Cataloguing in Publication Data

Main entry under title:

Private investigators

Catalogue of an exhibition held at the Walter Phillips Gallery.
Includes index.
ISBN 0-920159-61-3

1. Performance art—Alberta–Banff—Exhibitions. 2. Avant-guard (Aesthetics)—Exhibitions. 3. Arts, Modern—Alberta—Banff–Exhibitions. I. Chen, Millie. II. Crowston, Catherine. III. Maclear, Kyo Iona, 1970- IV. Walter, Kathryn. V. Walter Phillips Gallery.

NX513.B36P74 1999   700'.97123'32   C98-910986-0

Book and cover design by Michelle Teran
Private Investigators is a project by Kathryn Walter

Photo credits: Tanis Booth: 33, 42; *Canadian Gazette*: 23; Canadian Pacific Archives Image No. A.6189: x; Glenbow Museum Archives 2595: 17; Kathy Kennedy: 72-73, 77; Don Lee/The Banff Centre for the Arts: cover (front and back) iii, 4-5, 18, 19, 30, 31, 35, 37, 39, 41, 44, 45, 58, 59, 70, 71; Kathryn Walter: 8, 21, 27, 47, 49, 53, 61-67, 73 (bottom), 74; Whyte Museum of the Canadian Rockies, NA 65-140: 25.

We gratefully acknowledge the support of the Canada Council for the Arts for our publishing program.

Banff Centre Press
The Banff Centre for the Arts
Box 1020-50
Banff, Alberta Canada TOL OCO
tel (403) 762-7532 fax (403) 762-6699
http://www.banffcentre.ab.ca/Writing/Press/index.html

The Banff Centre
for the Arts

Contents

Acknowledgements

An event that takes place over the course of three weeks, every day full of action and reaction, requires the commitment and cooperation of an energetic crew. In the case of this project, new works were created by participating artists, an exhibition was installed, photo shoots were staged, documentation was printed, a video was produced and publicity was circulated, all on-site and within this limited time frame. I thank all the artists—Millie Chen, Shawna Dempsey, Faye HeavyShield, Kathy Kennedy, Lorri Millan, Shelley Niro, Judy Radul and Evelyn Von Michalofski—for their outstanding work and for their confidence, respect and sense of humour in meeting the demands of this intensive event. They join me in thanking the staff at the Walter Phillips Gallery, especially Mimmo Maiolo, Debra Reeve and MJ Thompson for their ingenuity and resourcefulness. In the Media and Visual Arts Department, we thank Tanis Booth for her organization and enthusiasm, Don Lee for his portrait photography and versatility, and resident Sandy Stone for her wit and good humour. In addition, Shawna Dempsey and Lorri Millan thank Noreen Stevens and Susan Chafe. Judy Radul thanks Oliver Hockenhull, Mimmo Maiolo, Dan David, Dave Mackenzie, Colin Funk and Gustavo Artigas. Millie Chen and Evelyn von Michalofski thank Sara Kirk and Kelley Russell. Shelley Niro thanks Ernie Kroeger. And Kathy Kennedy thanks Theresa Leonard, Martin Finnerty, Erin Michie and Rhonda Jessen. I extend a special thanks to Catherine Crowston for hosting this project, for coordinating a tremendous crew from The Banff Centre for the Arts and for her continued support throughout the course of events. Finally, this book could not have been produced without the dedication of the artists and Kyo Maclear, whose contributions reflect the spirit of the project. I thank Nancy Campbell and Cathy Busby for their comments on various drafts of my texts, Alison Reid for her support and thorough edit, Michelle Teran for her thoughtful design, and Lori Burwash and Lauri Seidlitz at the Banff Centre Press for bringing it all together.

—*Kathryn Walter*

Foreword

Catherine Crowston

The Walter Phillips Gallery and The Banff Centre for the Arts are set in picturesque Banff National Park, ringed by the majestic Rocky Mountains, yet surrounded too by contradictions. Each year, the "pristine wilderness" of the park is traversed by more than four million tourists who leave behind a trail of footprints, refuse and credit-card receipts. In effect, the stores that line Banff Avenue displace attention from the real object being consumed—the image of nature carefully packaged as a tourist commodity.

Ideas of objectification, commodification and consumption are not foreign to most women. It is appropriate, then, that for the exhibition *Private Investigators*, guest curator Kathryn Walter invited women artists to address the contradictions of Banff specifically, but also to extend this investigation into the roles we all play in maintaining society's imperatives. The usefulness of masquerade and disguise are well known to women, whose histories and experiences have often been obscured or misrepresented. The artists in *Private Investigators*, through subtle acts that paradoxically conceal and reveal, reclaim what has been lost, hidden or made invisible.

I would like to thank Kathryn Walter for the ideas behind this project. It was a major undertaking, and her energy and commitment were endless. It was also my great pleasure to work with each of the artists—Millie Chen, Shawna Dempsey, Faye HeavyShield, Kathy Kennedy, Lorri Millan, Shelley Niro, Judy Radul and Evelyn Von Michalofski—over the course of the *Private Investigators* project. I am appreciative of their creativity, generosity and ongoing friendship.

I am, as ever, deeply grateful to the staff of the Walter Phillips Gallery for making the performances and exhibition such a success, particularly to Heather Klassen, MJ Thompson, Mimmo Maiolo and Debra Reeve. It is most enjoyable to work with such a dedicated and talented group of people.

A project of this scale and duration cannot happen without the contribution of many individuals and departments within the Banff Centre. Gallery staff were assisted by production associate Tanis Booth, student interns Sara Kirk and Kelly Russell and the entire staff of the Media and Visual Arts Department. I would like to thank Don Lee for the hours of photography; the video crew—Richard Agecoutay, Jed DeCory, Aubrey Fernandez and Steve Nixon—for documenting the performances, exhibition and cabaret; Rhonda Jessen, Ernie Kroeger and Tara Neish for their support of the artists, and the department of Technical Services—Mark Richardson, Chris Segnitz, Lee Thompson and Ben West—for their enthusiastic participation.

I would also like to thank the staff of the Theatre Arts department for their assistance with the exhibition. Over the course of the summer, we borrowed props, equipment, space and staff time, and the project was greatly enhanced by their spirit of cooperation. Finally, on behalf of the Walter Phillips Gallery, I would like to acknowledge the assistance of the Canada Council for the Arts for their contribution to both the exhibition and publication. Their ongoing support of the Gallery makes such projects possible.

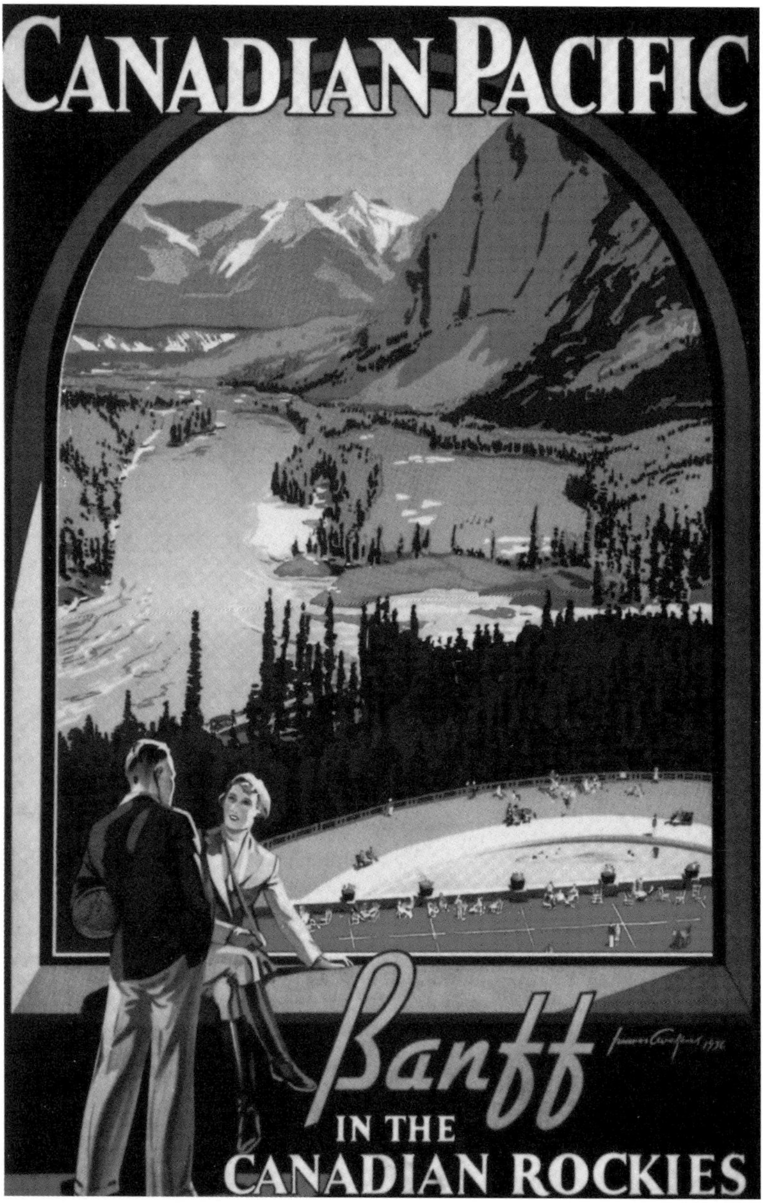

Canadian Pacific—Banff in the Canadian Rockies.
Artist: James Crockart, 1936.

Introduction

Kathryn Walter

The Set

Banff, an Alberta town in the Bow River Valley, Rocky Mountains.
The main street is lined with boutiques and candy stores, sports bars and shops.
Signs read Currency Exchange, Souvenirs, Paris Restaurant, Alberta Beef.

Banff was founded in frontier fashion when an economically fertile plot of land was cleared and a stage was set for a colonial story to take its course. In the 1880s, the Canadian Pacific Railway claimed this site as a tourist stop on the transcontinental line that forged through the mountains and laid the foundation for a future of progress and fortune. This settlement, which began as a small but prosperous government townsite, has grown into a pastiche of late-twentieth-century commercial development centred on a main street, extending outward into parceled private lots with the pretence of authentic European experience: Swiss, Alpine and Tudor chalets are the backdrop for a play featuring speculation and consumption through which the mercantile model of the past has achieved corporate proportion. Each year thousands of tourists from far and away flock to this glittering oasis in nature's rugged midst where the landscape, *the big attraction*, is reproduced in fragments and packaged for sale. Visitors enter this set in search of a holiday, led by their desires, constrained only by the limits of their pocketbooks and leisure time.

You can be what you want to be in the land of opportunity!

The Situation

The Private Investigators (PIs) were a number of artists—Millie Chen, Evelyn Von Michalofski, Shawna Dempsey, Lorri Millan, Kathy Kennedy, Faye HeavyShield, Shelley Niro and Judy Radul—invited to the Banff Centre for three weeks to create new work. My intention as curator of the exhibition was to bring these artists together to consider the concept of masquerade and to invent characters or roles to be performed in and around Banff. The artists took different perspectives on the site, and the project evolved into "a passage of a few people through a rather brief moment in time."[1] I borrow this phrase from the title of the ICA retrospective exhibition of the Situationist International as an apt description of this event, and as a reference to the idea of cultural practice as a form of social critique—in particular, a critique of the society of spectacle.[2]

Banff was the ideal site for my intentions. As a tourist town, it combines an itinerant population with a consumer's paradise, and as a cultural locus, it is home to the Banff Centre, where artists live in residence and work on-site with access to material resources. This situation allowed the artists to inspire and support one another, creating a social milieu that was both critical and pleasurable, generating energy that made the show a "happening" thing. My contributions varied with respect to the whole project as a creative endeavour—taking pictures and notes as well as facilitating, negotiating and, admittedly, vicariously participating.

The project involved taking risks, as it emphasized process and integrated viewer responses into the works. The performances acquired meaning as they were accepted or rejected under public scrutiny. Though the artists arrived with their attire and a plan of attack, none of their characters had previously been made public. The level of experimentation was high. Staging and posing were part of the PIs' interventions, and making irony and parody—even moments of travesty—were conscious strategies for social engagement. In many cases, assumptions about audience reactions were inaccurate, reinforcing the reality that the so-called public is various and unpredictable, defying preconceptions and unitary definitions.

The performances took place in and around town, and the Walter Phillips Gallery was used as an exhibition space and a documentation centre. The front space of the gallery served as a project room where the artists installed workstations, including props appropriate to their characters' interactions. This room was painted red, and a large mirror surrounded by vanity lights hung on the end wall, creating the semblance of a theatre dressing room. Here, the PIs stored their costumes and hung photo-documentation of their Banff performances. Journal entries and log-book excerpts were pinned to the walls or assembled on a desk. The project room was like a change room, and a room that changed during the three weeks that the artists were in residence. Following our stay, this space remained as we had left it for the duration of the exhibition. Here, viewers could not avoid reflections of themselves and one another in the mirror. They too became performers caught in the act of seeing and being seen.

Notes

1. The exhibition *on the passage of a few people through a rather brief moment in time: The Situationist International 1957–72* was organized by Peter Wollen and Mark Francis with Paul-Hervé Parsy, in consultation with Thomas Y. Levin, Greil Marcus and Elizabeth Sussman, and produced by the Institute of Contemporary Art, Boston, in collaboration with the Centre Georges Pompidou, Paris, 1989. The Situationist International (SI) were a group of European intellectuals committed to the critique of consumerism and commodity culture through theoretical, political and artistic means. They lived and worked in Paris in the 1950s and 60s and have influenced cultural practice in Europe and North America.

2. *The society of spectacle* is a term used by the SI writer Guy Debord to describe the ways that lived experience is represented through commercial images and mass media—a late-capitalist landscape of images that overdetermine social codes and behaviours and channel desire into consumption. The SI sought to destabilize and rupture these signs of the spectacle by constructing situations, events and happenings, using the street as an arena for art and politics.

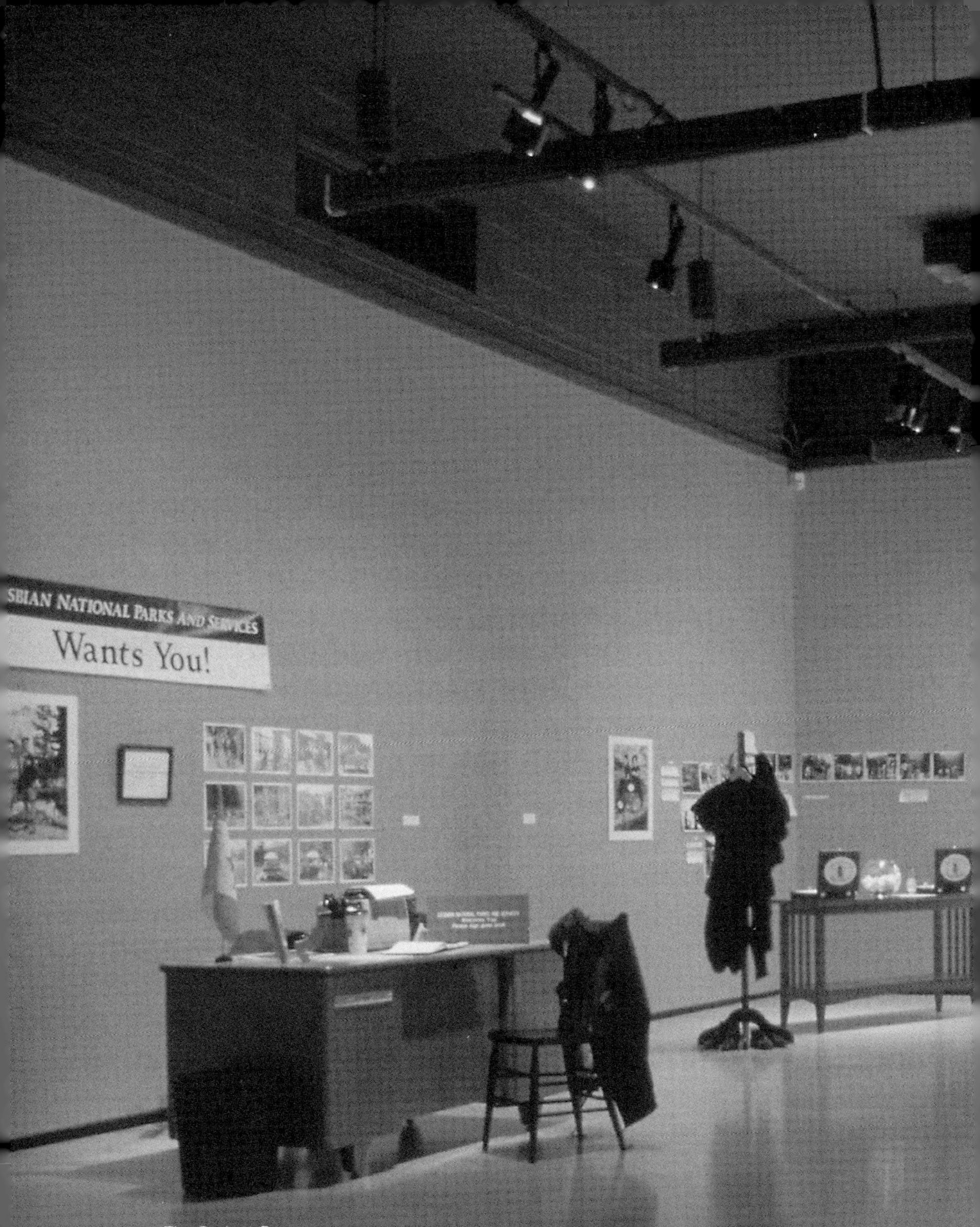

The Project Room:
Lesbian National Parks & Services Headquarters
Oracle Brand booth
Old Sister/New Sister work station
The Specialists
(pictured left to right)

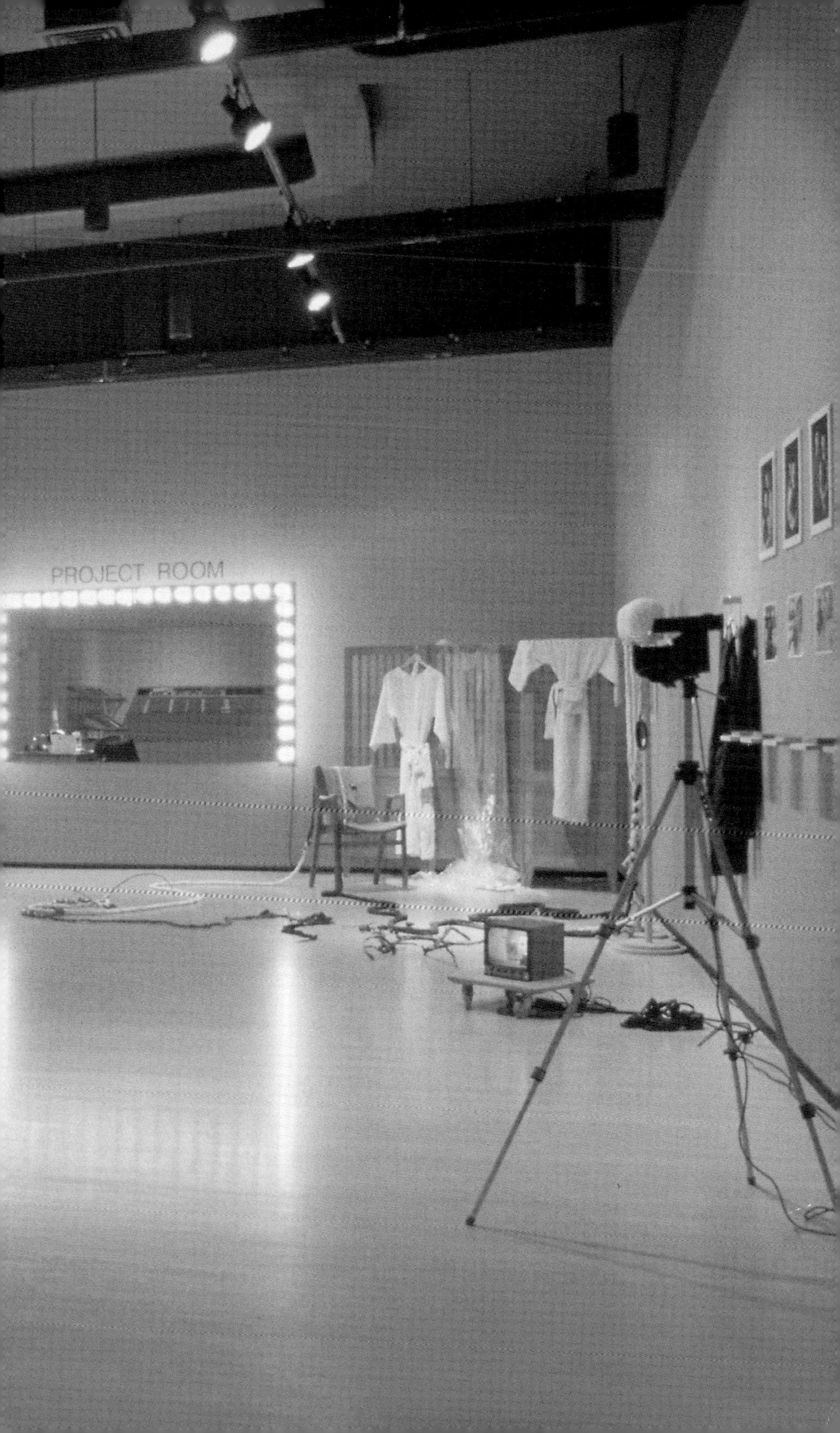
PROJECT ROOM

The Cast of Characters

Shawna Dempsey and **Lorri Millan** have collaborated full-time since 1989 on many performance, video and publication projects in diverse venues—theatres, community centres, art galleries and the street. This inspiring pair is well known for their *Dress Series* (1989–97), a collection of performances that send up female stereotypes. They have developed a signature stage style, with monologues written by Shawna and Lorri and performed by Shawna. In Banff, both artists were visible, flipping their femme side in the roles of Rangers for the *Lesbian National Parks & Services*.

Millie Chen and **Evelyn Von Michalofski** have worked collaboratively on several projects that cross lines between visual art and performance. Their costume-based works focus on viewer interaction, as in *Yurtopia* (1995), a mock-anthropological study that involved constructing a yurt using fibres collected from households and industries in the communities around southern Alberta. Their good-natured attempts at audience engagement unfortunately, though interestingly, backfired on them during their encounters in Banff. *Oracle Brand* proved to be an enlightening, though somewhat cynical, investigation into the private "public" spaces of this tourist town.

Shelley Niro is known for her photographs and films that narrate and portray exchanges and conflicts between Western and First Nations cultures. Her sassy humour is evident in her high-spirited photo series *Mohawks in Beehives* (1990–92). Shelley the Private Investigator invited **Faye HeavyShield**, who is originally from the Blood Reserve near Calgary, to collaborate with her. Faye's work is similar to Shelley's in content, but her minimalist installations have a very different style. *She: A Room Full of Women* (1994), among other works, uses women's clothing to reflect spiritual influences from Aboriginal and European traditions. In Banff, these two artists developed their first collaboration, combining their experiences as artists and as First Nations women. *Old Sister/New Sister* united Shelley's humour and Faye's use of material in a performance with poignancy and punch.

Judy Radul has worked principally as a performance artist on stage, but her recent work includes a drag routine called *My Guy* (1995), which was played out and photographed in the streets of Vancouver. As the back-street boy in that piece, she was as convincing as she was in the femme fatale character she played in Banff. Taking a position different from that of the other artists, Judy interpreted masquerade as an exploration from within, using the conventions of the already-existing, pervasive role of the heterosexual consumer, and casting five men as her accomplices. *The Specialists* was a subtle conceptual intervention that made the unsuspecting crowd suspect.

Kathy Kennedy has orchestrated several ambitious performance pieces with large groups of people, including the women's choir Choer Maha and a series of "sonic parades" in public places. She is founder of Studio XX in Montreal, an outlet that provides women with free access to technological resources. She was the resident techno-PI in Banff, where she created a Web site with an interface of windows that hid her own identity amid a series of real and fictitious personae. During her stay, she also wrote and conducted one of her sonic parades down Banff Avenue, stirring up community action and reaction.

It was fortuitous to encounter **Kyo Maclear** during our stay at the Banff Centre. She was participating in the Arts Journalism residency, a program running concurrently with the summer exhibitions, and she frequently attended public presentations. Always quick on the draw during question periods, she would offer keen insights that suggested she would be the ideal candidate for the articulate witness. I asked her to write about the Private Investigators for this publication, and she has contributed her eyewitness accounts and her witty musings as innocent bystander. Kyo has worked as a writer and editor for various art and culture publications.

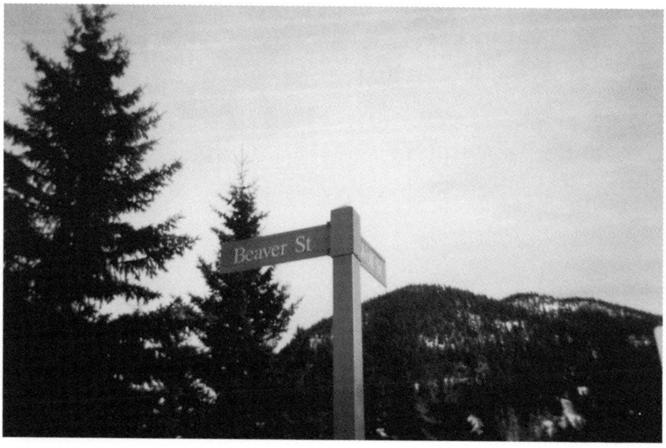
Beaver St

The Accidental Witness

Kyo Maclear

I spot Shawna and Lorri standing by the dessert table in the dining hall, considering the apple strudel and chocolate mousse. They wear the same tan uniforms I would see them in for the next three weeks. From a distance, their green badges are illegible—to the unwitting observer, they could be health inspectors doing their rounds, no more or less out of place in the gentrified cafeteria than any of the other diners. But rumour has preceded them, and I have been alerted to their presence: "Look: the Lesbian Park Rangers," my colleague announces.

My first sighting of the Banff masqueraders occurred a mere three days after I had arrived at the Centre to participate in the annual Arts Journalism residency. Little did I know when I stuffed my notes, diskettes and clothes into my duffel bag what lay in store.

During the course of my month-long stay, Shawna Dempsey and Lorri Millan would invite residents and daytrippers to unpack their conceptual baggage about the Canadian wilderness. They would be joined by six other costumed artists—Faye HeavyShield, Shelley Niro, Evelyn Von Michalofski, Millie Chen, Kathy Kennedy and Judy Radul—each recruited as a "private investigator" by the guest curator, Kathryn Walter, each employing a docudrama approach to create fictional situations with "real" people. A sound parade down the main street, a Lesbian Rangers recruitment day, an Oracle Brand soap giveaway were among the unusual situations people encountered that July in Banff.

While conceived separately, the "events"—or site gags—emphasized the artifice of sight-seeing, homing in on endemic preconceptions that shape the scripts for our travels. Visitors to Banff were reminded in myriad ways that we partake of the commodities, vanities and ideologies associated with tourism.

A happy-trails mentality invites social amnesia. Highway signs should read Beware of Canada's Natural and Pictorial Legends! They Ambush History! (Without leaping into the archives, how are Banff initiates to know that the land they walk on is part of a Siksika Nation land claim ... that the Rockies served as a physical and symbolic border for Japanese Canadians who were not allowed west of the mountains until the late 1940s ... that the peaks are unmarked graves for Chinese railroad labourers who *died in the thousands*?) Countless legacies and multiple "others" have gone MIA; certain histories have become subterranean. Why? Because as "ecotourists" we are encouraged to travel with our heads in the clouds, our eyes fixed on the stars, our feet on the forest paths before us. The irony is that in travel literature the Canadian landscape is celebrated for its grandeur and fecundity. (Canada could top the Fortune 500 List if nature counted as an investment holding!) Yet when it comes to imagining the past—or, for that matter, the social present—the same guidebooks make a virtue of being *resource-poor*. We *turistas* are encouraged to be flat broke on thought, dizzy on the scenery, as we indulge our wanderlust. Banff's spectatorial aids—its postcards, pamphlets, natural museums and monuments—continue to stone us on beauty and apathy. Every time we fancy ourselves first-time explorers, every moment we imagine that our presence is in some way *inaugural*, we assent to this collective hallucination.

The Private Investigators incisively exposed the peril of unthinking tourism with the goal of developing a critical perspective on its hidden costs and assumptions. Their *modus operandi* was to go incognito, to avoid any This Is Art pronouncements as they went interloping and sleuthing in disguise. They chose to spotlight tourism's usual suspects: variously posing as park wardens, wilderness ghosts, tour guides and holiday shoppers to recontextualize the clichés of peak season. Real-life tourists were cast as extras (some consciously, others unwittingly) in the unfolding dramas. As the plot for each performance thickened, attention was drawn to Banff's historic inhabitants, its ongoing social divisions, the uses and abuses of its land, its increased commercialism and the experience of nature that has made a "return" to it so obstructed by colonial mythology.

"A forest shares a history which each tree remembers even after it has been felled," writes Anne Michaels. A reissued collection of her poetry was among the books I packed for my residency. I liked that line, so I penned it in my journal. I made other journal entries during my stay in Banff, not knowing that I'd be returning to them months later in an effort to reconstruct "eyewitness" accounts of the *Private Investigator* performances. Tonight, as I reread certain passages, it is clear that many of my initial impressions of Banff—the tourist destination and performance site—have since been retouched. Call it hindsight. The larger story I create around "what happened, what I saw" continues to change such that the narrative of "my travels" spins out without an assignable end point. Even if I attempt to remain utterly faithful to my original memories, the patient task of piecing together what has been scattered invariably creates new meanings. (Of course, I realize that travel experiences may be mythologized by repetition into well-wrought chapters of our lives—hence family slide shows that get annual reruns—but I find this prospect so sad and unimaginative that I prefer to believe that memories are better left unfixed.) So tonight, as I look back, the significance of my often ineloquent journal notes rests in what they may reveal to me about travel writing, which, like travel itself, is based on an alloy of fact and fiction. Memories, I know, at once eliminate and embellish. They travel too.

July 2, 1997. On the day I am scheduled to arrive for the residency, my friends drive me from Calgary to Banff in a covered Jeep. With a map and schedule to fix our itinerary, we wend our way towards the Banff Centre. As a newcomer, I have been given the "observation" seat.

Everything I can see out of the bug-splattered window suggests an expanse, a continuity that forces me to be aware of, to trace, the length of our noisy ride over it. The light, the air, the gradation of colour all play a part in the sequence. It is, as they say, *breathtaking*. A photogenic landscape without blemishes, it fulfills every guidebook description. In fact, because a panorama is about overall impressions, there is really no need for me to try to watch closely or become absorbed in details of my view. To participate, I need only check from time to time that it is all still going on. (Are the trees still whizzing by? Yup. Glittering lakes? Uh-huh.) Sight-seeing from a car is low-intensity involvement. No single scene or place matters very much. Looking is just passing by, punctuated by idle remarks like "Wow" or "Gosh."

As we near the hoodoos, my companions encourage me to focus on particulars. My first lesson in interrogating appearances happens as my friend turns down the blaring radio to draw my attention to ... Chinaman's Peak. *What did you call it?!* Chinaman's Peak, they tell me, will soon be renamed after a Chinese-Canadian mountain climber, the first person on record to reach its summit. The Alberta Historical Resources Foundation Board has conceded to arguments that the current name is racist and disparages the memory of workers who built the most dangerous sections of the railroad through the western mountains—in order to construct "Canada," tie by tie. I take heart in this information, but I have a nagging thought, which I finally decide to raise after a little throat clearing. *In the overall scheme of things ... I mean, what I'm trying to say is ... well, I just don't know if adding a Chinese name to those of Mount Douglas and Mount Rundle is much of an achievement.* There must be another way of honouring the memory of Chinese workers, whose identities and labour were rendered invisible, than by scratching new names on outcroppings of the continental crust?

The land is turning out to be much more volatile and controversial an issue than guidebooks like Fodor's would have us believe. Not that this is a revelation. Whether or not we choose to realize it, Banff is cross-hatched with histories, which tell of migrants traversing great distances and early inhabitants who travelled no distance whatsoever, all enduring unspeakable difficulty or oppression. The unbroken vista reveals its faultlines, like fissures in ore. Although such landscape and its toponyms encourage an active recognition of history, an emotional fathoming of all the memories tucked into nature's awesomeness, only some stories have been selected for perpetuation.

Our Jeep has reached the Banff Centre. As Ernest Hemingway would have it: The sun sets. We arrive. Or Jack Kerouac: We skid into the joint, rubber screaming—we're here!

July 5, 1997. This morning I woke up thinking I was back home. I lay there in a slipstream of thoughts, parched and clueless. Eyelids finally lifted, I travel towards the morning light, opening the balcony door to step outside. My sleepy gaze ricochets over the trees, drifts down to the valley, across the silver horizon, the rugged snow-capped mountains, wandering aimlessly, like a radar beam disconnected from the viewing tube in a control tower. I see a wave of slopes and crags. Mount Rundle looks like a shark's tooth gnawing on the clouds, I think. A gigantic mass before me.

On postcards sold in town, the spectacular mountain images contribute to the canon of scenic splendour, CANADA writ large. It transmits a comforting message of grandeur to those who succumb to the idea that Canadians, unlike Americans, are too moderate to extol domestic merit. Those Canucks who fear our very identity is in danger of obliteration by the juggernaut to the south—those who fear that McBanff burgers and Mount Rundle Dairy Queen sundaes are just around the corner—can leave Banff flush with local colour, "authentic" Indian curios and, perhaps most important, a sense of BIGNESS. To be in the Rockies, after all, is to be released from the grasp of understatement. Not only are commercial hyperbole and the hype of tourism welcome, but they are socially *expected*.

As a vista, an abstraction, Banff is unmatched in national iconography. Quite literally, it must be the most looked at emblem of Canada. (How many postcards of the Rockies are at this moment on how many walls?) The propaganda is so effective, so international, that despite my protests to the contrary, my Japanese relatives remained convinced that I lived in a Swiss-style chalet well into the late 1970s. They used to send me woollen socks, in case I suffered frostbite as I leaped through the snow in my parka. It wasn't naiveté alone that contributed to their perception of Canada as a winter wonderland, it was the pervasiveness of a BIG idea. The idea persists, albeit in diluted form, only now it is more efficiently distributed via global electronic networks. It continues, as Private Investigators Millie and Evelyn remind us, to constitute a particular ideology, one that originally emerged from the combined interests of exploration and exploitation.

Meanwhile, the theme of Western ruggedness has been transformed into a series of self-aggrandising images, available to people with padded wallets. (The superior viewpoint promises to create gods out of mere mortals. What better place to go if you want to feel on top of the world?) Arriving in Banff means crossing into a world of superlative sentiment. Everything has been appropriated as scenery, decorated with uncomplicated adjectives.

As a lesson in the near-impossible, I ask five friends to describe Banff's vista in ten words or less without using the descriptives *beautiful*, *grand* or *rugged*. Write it as if you were writing copy for a postcard, I tell them. Can you interpret the landscape to reveal more than the generic, archetypal platitudes? What I get in response is at once enigmatic and poetic. Indicating Banff's contemporary attractions and frustrations, my friends situate the land in a socio-historical context, showing how human traffic and technology are part of the local ecology. Their words suggest a non-profit language. I welcome them as an antidote to the genteel and mercenary boredom of "tourish."

Adjectives franchised in flesh a shudder of ice-age rigor mortis. —B.J.

Rundle, forest, bow, springs, elk, visa/mastercard preferred but interac accepted. —A.M.

Tranquility broken, one could hurl rocks onto dumbass disruptive tourists. —D.D.

It crouches under Sleeping Buffalo Mountain. Does the buffalo dream? —M.A.

Mata mata koko ni kita. —T.T.

Tourism is about positive self-representation. It is a masquerade based on smiling texts, social forgetfulness and polite displacement. A tourist pamphlet for Bergen-Belsen, Nanking or My Lai would seem anomalous, even obscene. While such things undoubtedly exist, they are rare because the symbolic economies of commemoration and tourism are frequently positioned as incompatible. (Call it ethics or, more cynically, market segmentation.) Tourists generally want an assurance of superficiality, an implicit guarantee that the culture, people and places they visit will not challenge their preconceptions, upset their peace of mind. Tourism, in its accepted forms, is not meant to topple the social hierarchy or account for the extent of cultural translation required to cross geopolitical lines. One does not ordinarily go to Acapulco to look into the labour practices of multinationals, to Kuala Lumpur to inquire about the impact of recent forest fires; one is on vacation. (Isn't the idea to return rested and sated? To delve into local hamlets by day and settle into the local Hilton by night?)

But unexpected things happen. A tourist looks at a mountain range and expects stasis. Suddenly a rock dislodges, tumbling in the direction of a parked bus, and that same person is now an eyewitness. Sometimes you have no other choice but to watch something unsettling occur. To paraphrase the artist Jenny Holzer, you don't have the option of closing your eyes because it happens fast and enters your memory.

Let's just say that in my own case, metaphoric boulders were whizzing by me throughout my Banff residency. Nothing so devasting as a bus collision occurred, but in a different way I became an accidental witness, straggling behind the peripatetic investigators as they explored the dynamics of exclusion in the area and advised passersby to mind the commercial bunk, to dig up the dirt on local history. My viewing presence—my intentions, blindness and sight—became part of the witnessing activity.

I was also a tourist in Banff. As it happens, the subgroup to which I belong, artists and writers, takes a rather deluded pride in its detachment from commercial culture. It appears to be important for us to feel unaffiliated with tourist/bourgeois values. But many of us remain nettled, despite our sense of immunity. When I spread suntan lotion and bug spray over my body, take out the more summery of my dresses from a suitcase and my hiking boots from the closet, pay for postcards at La Palette, speaking English to the francophone cashier, my bank card, my boutique-bought dress and sporty footwear and my unflappable manners are so many props in the theatre of tourism. It would be foolish and, worse, ahistorical, to attempt to erase my itinerant presence. A politics of tourism means that I am accountable for my travelling activities, no matter how innocent or private they may seem.

July 30, 1997. I wander into the Walter Phillips Gallery on the day of my departure. The Private Investigators' uniforms are hung in the gallery during off-hours, waiting for the next tour through Banff. Some are draped on hangers, others on mannequins. Because I am looking at them now as artifacts, I notice more how the tailoring of each outfit defines the body, creating different rules for movement, even for shifting body parts (like breasts in a bodice). While the clothing has been invested with new meanings and intents, each costume signifies an identity under construction—one that can be put on and removed without trace or memory.

Behind the clothing, the gallery walls are crowded with photos documenting the performances as they occurred. They are reproduced in this book to give readers—and belated witnesses—a *partial* portrait of what happened. I stress the word *partial* because that's the only view they can offer. No matter how idiosyncratic the photos, how much they hint at actual events, they cannot help tacitly simplifying what took place. The inimitable quirks and details of each performance have been dispersed, along with their participants. I think this is why I decide to pen a few postcards before I leave. "Wish you were here!" I write in all earnestness before slipping the cards into a mailbox and exiting the scene.

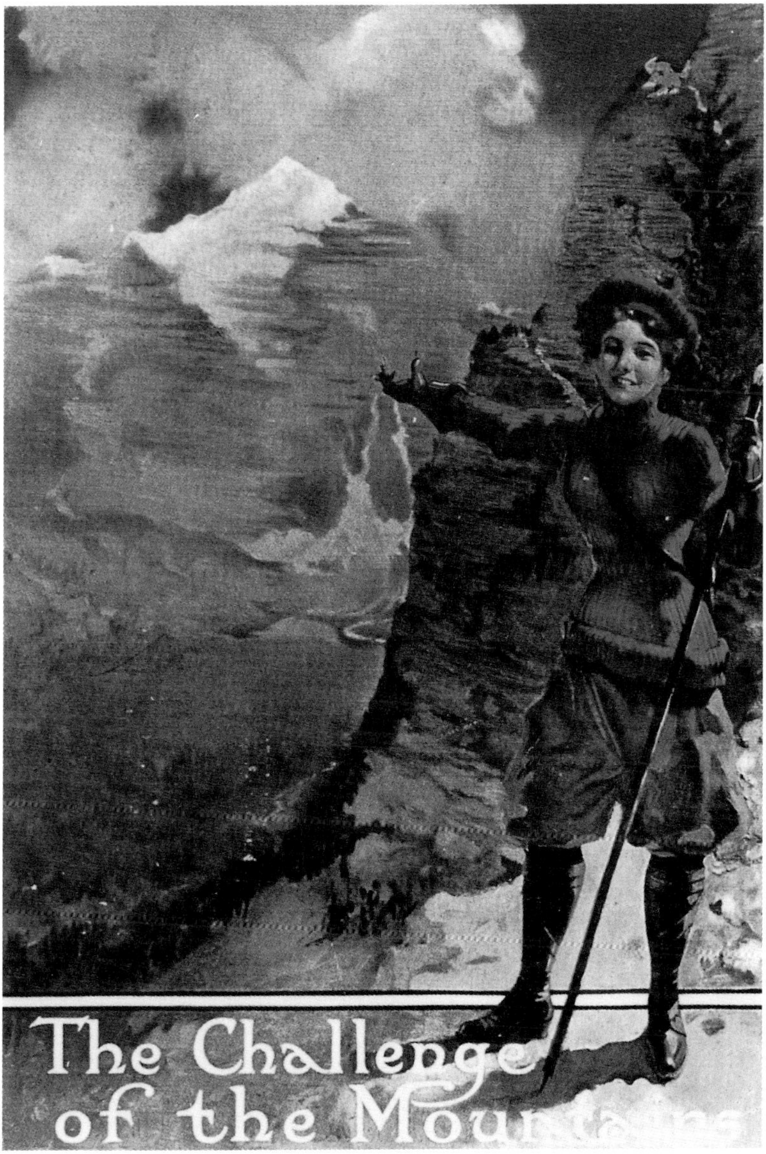

"Alpine Annie" in the Canadian Rockies.

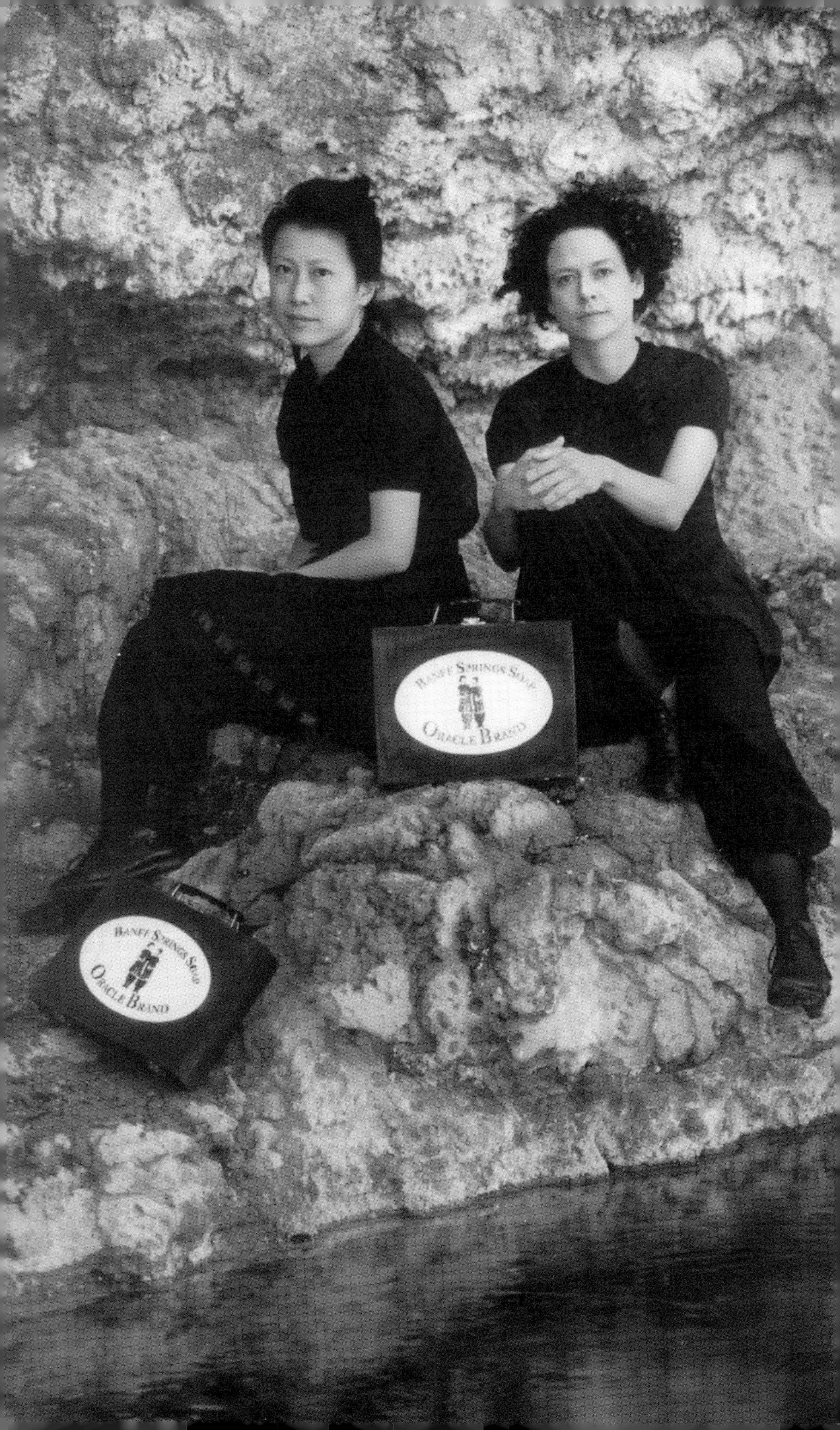
BANFF SPRINGS SOAP
ORACLE BRAND
BANFF SPRINGS SOAP
ORACLE BRAND

Oracle Brand

SCENARIO

The Cave and Basin National Historic Site documents the story of three white railway workers who in 1883 reportedly "discovered" the hot springs that proved to be the jewel of the Western Canadian landscape, the envy of entrepreneurs and the inspiration for the future fortune of Banff. "The Springs" appropriately became the name of the first tourist attraction, the luxury hotel built, owned and operated by Canadian Pacific Railway barons. Millie Chen and Evelyn Von Michalofski appropriated the mythology of discovery associated with this so-called founding and combined it with spiritual interpretations of divination in a performance called *Oracle Brand*. They adopted the role of soothsayer with a critical take on contemporary tourism.

Upon arrival at the Banff Centre, the artists began their production—a non-profit venture in the land of free enterprise. They acquired one thousand bars of hotel soap that they repackaged and labelled with their own design to create a product called Oracle Brand Banff Springs Soap. Enclosed with each bar was one of many fortunes critical of the developed landscape, forewarning and foreboding, prophetic and polemical comments on the transformation of the wilderness into capital. The artists packed their products into customized carrying cases stencilled with their invented trademark, and they wandered the streets and trails of Banff on a mission to give them away as souvenirs.

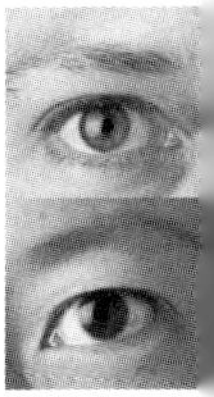

Millie and Evelyn designed their costumes based on fashion illustrations of Victorian bathers. The elegant black summer robes had a nostalgic aesthetic, a sombre look that set them apart from the Banff crowds clothed in Gore-Tex and spandex. Assumptions that they would be outshone by the quantity of neon colours around them were mistaken, as their black outfits claimed a lot of attention; perhaps they appeared to be cult members to unsuspecting tourists. The soothsayers were met with ungracious responses from people who assumed these characters were promoting some sub-religious business. *Their prophecies must be heresies* was the general impression. Despite their attractive dispositions, these characters were perceived as menaces to holiday seekers who had come to Banff to escape panhandlers, charity workers and door-to-door preachers. Their performance disrupted the flow of everyday consumption and challenged social convention.

In spite of the artists' concerted efforts to negotiate access to the Cave and Basin site through official channels, Millie and Evelyn were not allowed on the premises without authorized accompaniment. The Cave and Basin, now a museum celebrating the origin of Banff National Park, contains stagnant mineral pools, their levels maintained by pumps. This reservoir, which retains the sickly sweet smell of sulphur, stands as a backdrop to the reenactment of a story of progress, and disruptions to this narrative threaten popular belief.

The soothsayers were thus prevented from entering various venues, whether they requested permission or arrived unannounced. At the Sulphur Mountain gondola ride, their presence was immediately detected by authorities quick to respond to their surveillance systems. Millie and Evelyn had just opened their cases and passed out two bars of soap each when the manager of the gondola ride approached them angrily. They were apparently on private property, the limits of which were defined by a one-hundred-car parking lot, and they were asked to leave without delay. The proprietor of the gift shop clearly felt that *Oracle Brand* was infringing on her territory. Why would customers buy something from the gift shop if they could get a souvenir free? Giving something away was taboo in a town where even busking is prohibited. The soothsayers were committing a sin against the spirit of commerce.

Ironically, the performance we thought would be the most benign turned out to be the most disturbing. *Oracle Brand* became a private investigation of the ambiguous parameters between private and public space. Millie and Evelyn found that the most supposedly public places had the most protected borders.

After a series of hostile encounters, including a threat of being sued by the manager of the Banff Springs Golf Course, Millie and Evelyn became weary outlaws. Finally they decided to restrategize by setting up an Oracle Brand stand, and with this market-like system they successfully distributed their wares. More like merchants, they were less provocative; stationary, they were harmless. Poised at the view above the Banff Springs Hotel, on a lookout called Surprise Corner, they became a spectacle to be seen, swarmed by curious people looking for something to buy. Nevertheless, the artists continued to give away their critical fortunes, making subtle incursions into the consumer imagination.

—*Kathryn Walter*

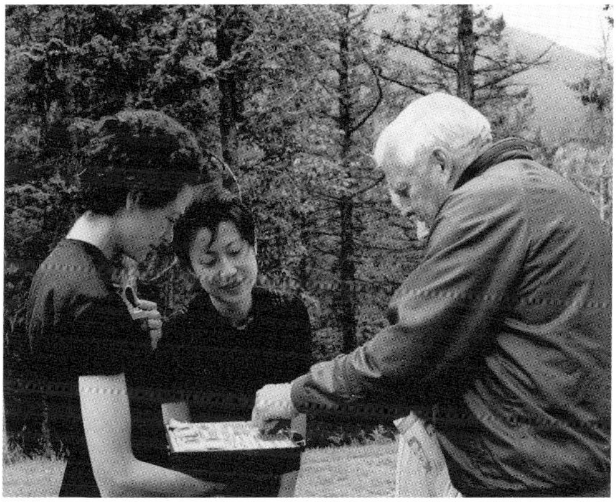

TM BANFF SPRINGS SOAP ORACLE BRAND®

You seek novel souvenirs to impress friends back home.

ORACLE BRAND BANFF SPRINGS SOAP™

Journal Excerpts

Monday, July 14, 1997

Parks Canada Administration Building:
Met with representative from Client Services of Parks Canada.
Sent us on paper chase to gain access to Cave and Basin historic site.
Very frustrating meeting in terms of degree of bureaucracy.
We are told that the public (i.e., tourists) must be protected from us.
We are left with the feeling that there is little comprehension of or desire to understand our intent and concept for this piece.
We are left feeling censored.

Banff Springs Hotel, Banff Springs Golf Course:
Chased off the golf course (even though we were careful to stay off the green) by Banff Springs Golf Course employee, "for our own safety": "golf ball in the head."
We gave the employee an Oracle Brand soap and he accepted it and even told us that we could peddle our soap souvenirs in the clubhouse—"just speak to the manager."
We are later suspicious that he was setting us up.
Didn't venture into the clubhouse.
Chased off the parking lot grounds by manager because we were placing soap souvenirs on car windshields.
Subsequently threatened with lawsuit for using "Banff Springs" on our packaging.

Tuesday, July 15, 1997

Banff Sulphur Mountain Gondola:
Chased off parking lot grounds by manager and gift shop manager.
Informed us that this is "private property," even though all property is leased from Parks Canada, which is supposed to be publicly owned.
Companies profit greatly from occupying this land.

NOTICE.

BANFF HOT SPRINGS!

The undersigned, under instructions from the the Honorable the Minister of the Interior, will be at Banff Springs on

THURSDAY, THE 24th DAY OF JUNE, INST.,

at 10 o'clock, A. M.,

And receive any evidence that parties may wish to offer in support of their claims as discoverers of said springs, or improvements made by them at said Springs.

All parties interested will please take notice and govern themselves accordingly.

W.M. PEARCE.

Calgary 7th June. 1886.

You are lured to the wilderness. Within the wilderness: 4 major highways, 1 railroad, 1 town, 1 hamlet, 1 golf course, 1 mini golf course, 1 bowling alley, 3 ski hills, 2,500 camp sites, 125 restaurants, 220 retail outlets, hotel accommodations and RV sites and convention centres and shopping malls for over 15,000 people, 20,000 traffic jams, 1 amusement park.

THE BANFF SPRINGS SOAP ORACLE BRAND®

ORACLE BRAND BANFF SPRINGS SOAP™

Wednesday, July 16, 1997 (noon)

Surprise Corner Lookout (with panoramic view of Banff Springs Hotel):

Tried the passive approach—worked much better.

People still suspicious of this gift giving—maybe we must rectify the imbalance of giving something away for nothing by asking for something in return—the economy of relationships.

Setting up by this favourite viewing and snapshot location gave people time to look us over and warm up to us (e.g., hike trail yesterday)—if at first they declined our offering, they had time to change their attitude or for their curiosity to be piqued.

Language/speech such an issue—Evelyn said of the Texans, "Maybe they don't speak English." The bus load of tourists whom I assumed were a Japanese tour group—at first so wary; such language and cultural barriers—until I heard Mandarin Chinese being spoken and I jumped in and they oohed and aahed and nodded and accepted our offerings with gratitude and excitement—"Aah! Art!"—and they waved goodbye from the bus.

So much more fulfilling, rewarding for us to engage in conversation with people.

Thursday, July 17, 1997 (noon)

Surprise Corner Lookout:

Power of belief: some people intensely mull over the divination categories, hesitate, ask for more than one divinatory soap because they have more than one wish—"by ghosts" "by walking in a circle" "by shadows or manes" "dreams" "by appearances in the air" "by dough of cakes."

Power of belief: some people refuse our offering because they don't want to be jinxed or receive bad prophecy—fear of future.

Suspension of disbelief—willingness and, in fact, desire to believe in the divination categories—(planting of clues), conjuring of dreams, illusion of magic, poetics of disillusionment.

Responsibility of translation of information—how responsible should we be in terms of other cultures' perceptions of us—not the same use of the ironic?

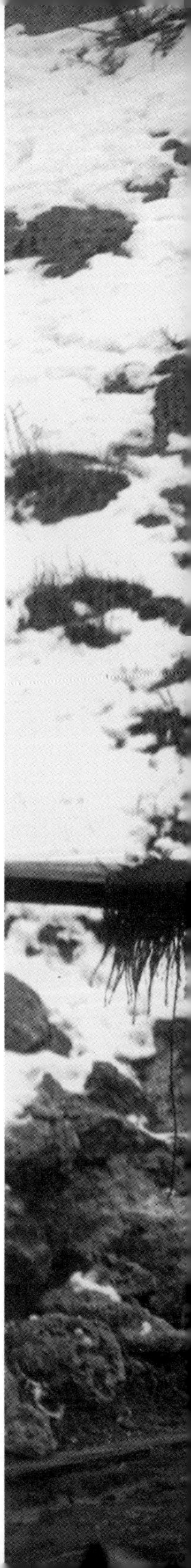

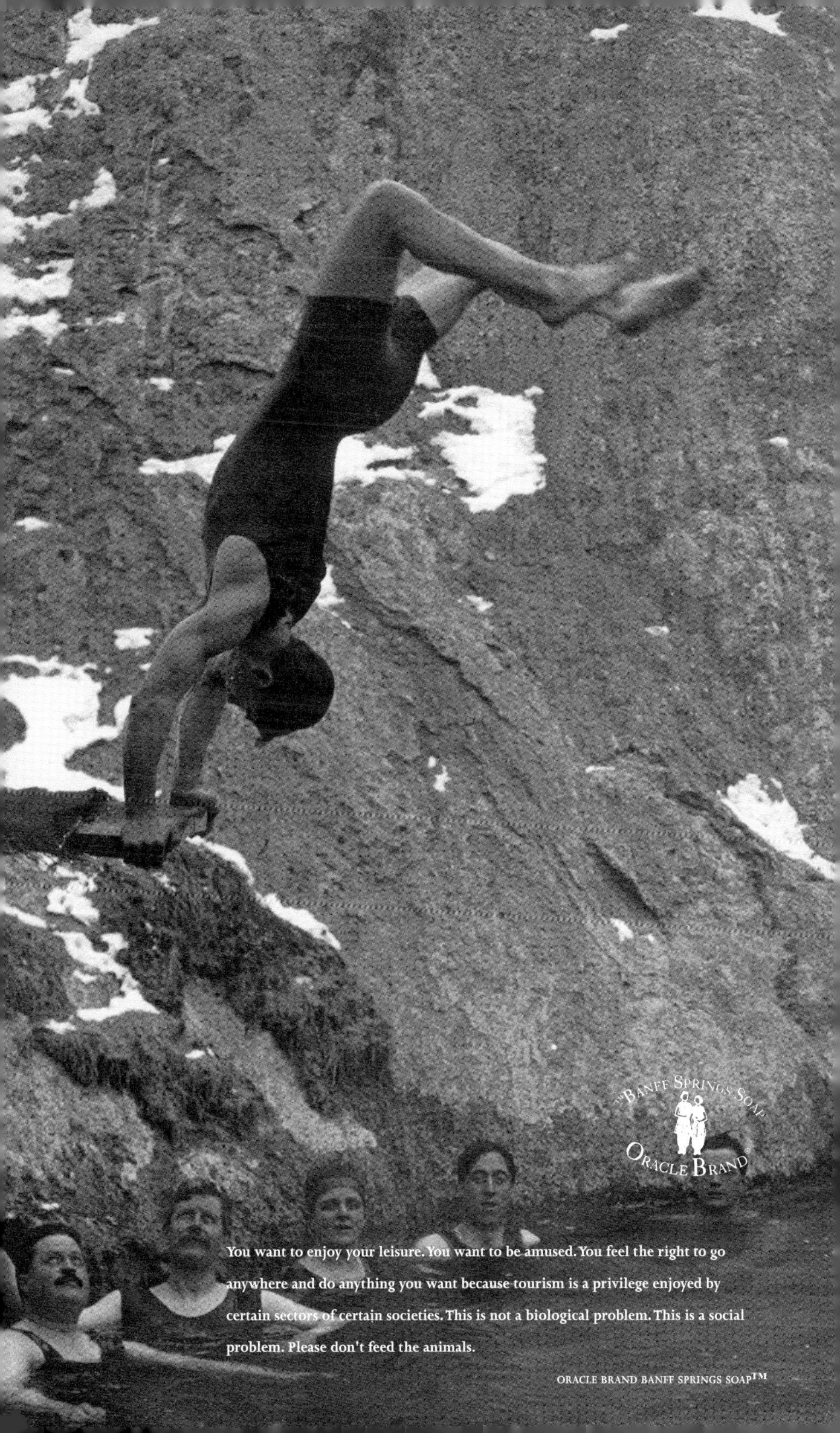
THE BANFF SPRINGS SOAP
ORACLE BRAND
You want to enjoy your leisure. You want to be amused. You feel the right to go anywhere and do anything you want because tourism is a privilege enjoyed by certain sectors of certain societies. This is not a biological problem. This is a social problem. Please don't feed the animals.
ORACLE BRAND BANFF SPRINGS SOAP™

Thursday, July 17, 1997 (afternoon)

Surprise Corner Lookout

Feeling guilty or irresponsible for being taken as legitimate soothsayers in the case of Japanese tourists.

One woman in particular is making me nervous: she doesn't seem to know that we're just posing as fortune-tellers; as she selects a soap from my case she repeats out loud, "Lucky, lucky, lucky."

I am also thinking about the totally different gift-giving culture of Japan; from what I understand, gift giving and receiving are intertwined with many levels of interpersonal familial business relationships in Japan.

I do not like the fact that I am incapable of explaining that it is not our intent to fool her or abuse her beliefs in prophecy.

We hope that the act of giving away free Oracle Brand soap may gently remind others that they are strangers here, that they are taking something away, perhaps something essential to the vital energy of the place. And that there are certain things that cannot be exchanged for dollars.

Millie Chen and Evelyn von Michalofski

You are standing in the middle of a "natural resource." You claim nature for your own use. This isn't a biological problem. This is a philosophical problem.

ORACLE BRAND BANFF SPRINGS SOAP™

™ Banff Springs Soap Oracle Brand®

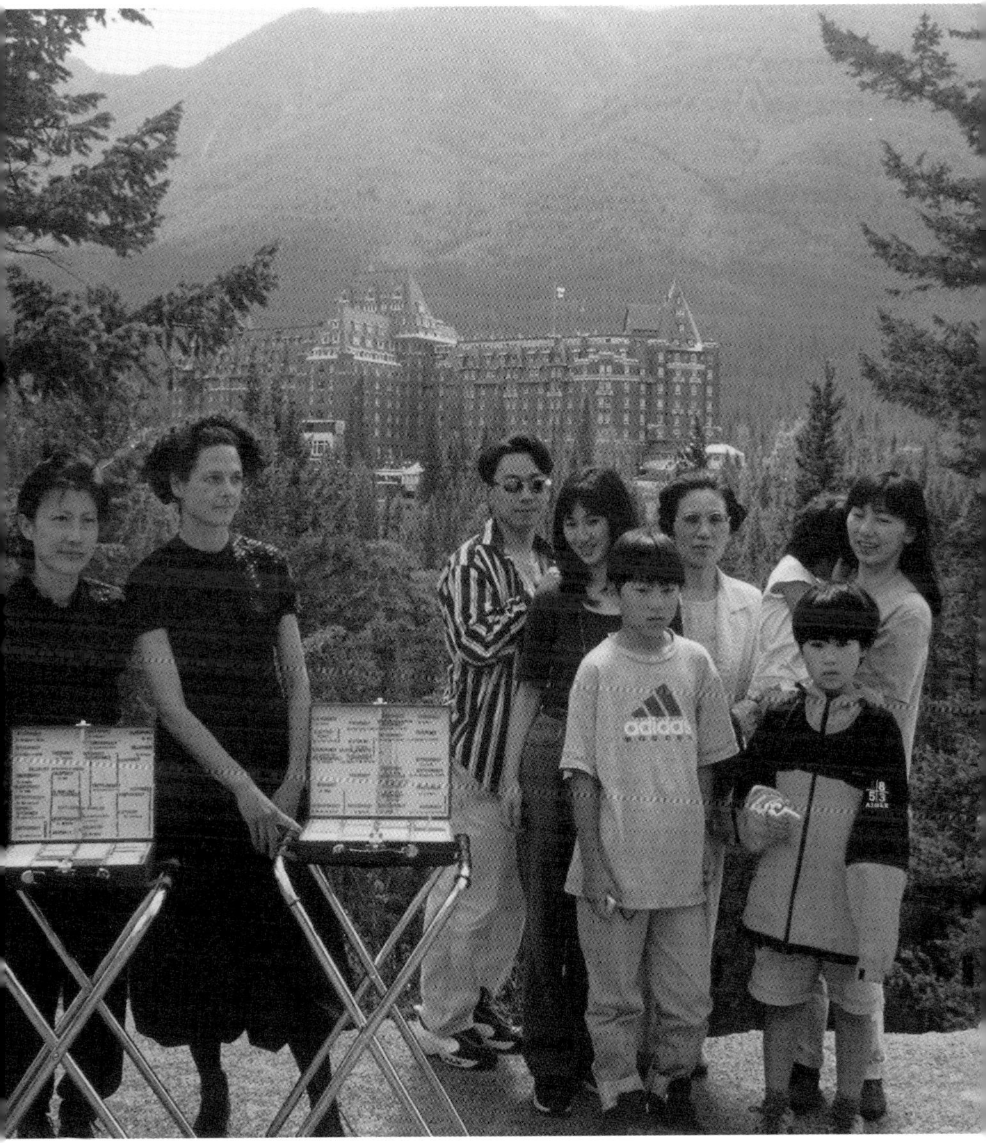
adidas

EYEWITNESS ACCOUNT

Millie Chen and Evelyn Von Michalofski appear austere in their black dresses. They tell me they are going for a cosmetic-salesgirl look, a straitlaced caricature of corporatism, but I'm not so sure. To me they look funereal, beauticians at a morgue. As their performance unfolds, I realize I hope to convince them that my perception of their appearance is not inappropriate. In fact, it seems befitting of a performance imbued with a sense of elegy.

Millie and Evelyn have, in essence, come to Banff to lament the treachery of scenic tourism. They have carefully prepared "oracles" to distribute to visitors along with dainty souvenir soap bars. The oracles offer a sombre litany of resource extraction and wildlife exploitation in the area—dating from the turn of the century when Banff was converted into a spa town for Europe's elite. Since that time, the Banff landscape has been hyped by advertising and disfigured by activity to encourage pleasure and profit. Tourists, as Millie and Evelyn opine, continue to leave wounds on the earth.

The Cave and Basin is the landmark site where three CPR workers allegedly discovered the Banff Hot Springs. Millie and Evelyn had hoped to use the venue for their *Oracle Brand* soap performance, but their plans were scuppered when they were refused a permit by authorities. Much to their chagrin, scuffles with Banff officials become a daily routine, making their performances infinitely more layered and certainly more mobile than they could ever have anticipated. Though Banff has a long tradition of boosterism, they are repeatedly chased away by security officers. They are screamed at by finger-wagging managers: no loitering! No vending!

A difficult start leads to other tensions. Misunderstandings, far from diminishing, actually escalate when the OB girls finally set up their soap stand and prepare to face their audience. The problem with their tourist-invader equation, they quickly realize, is that what was once a citadel of WASP gentility has become significantly more diverse. Katakana signs are propped in shop windows, and Chinese tourists alight from buses: the Banff tourist is no longer prototypically colonial, or, for that matter, even English-speaking. The *Oracle Brand* girls had counted on irony, shared cultural references, but many of the tourists are confused or suspicious. Millie and Evelyn feel guilty about conning several tourists into wholeheartedly believing their impersonation, wary of abusing the confidence of visitors who express genuine interest in the spiritual.

The initial frustration does not lead to failure. The *Oracle Brand* girls are quick-witted and flexible enough to adjust their expectations and eventually engage passing tourists more directly. And it is "all for good," as they say. Through their upsets and triumphs, Millie and Evelyn confront the issue facing all performance artists: that of audience. They know that without an audience, a soapbox is just more detritus for the recycling bin.

—*Kyo Maclear*

You are on an island of wilderness surrounded by a sea of civilization. In the future, every activity will feed into tourism.

ORACLE BRAND BANFF SPRINGS SOAP™

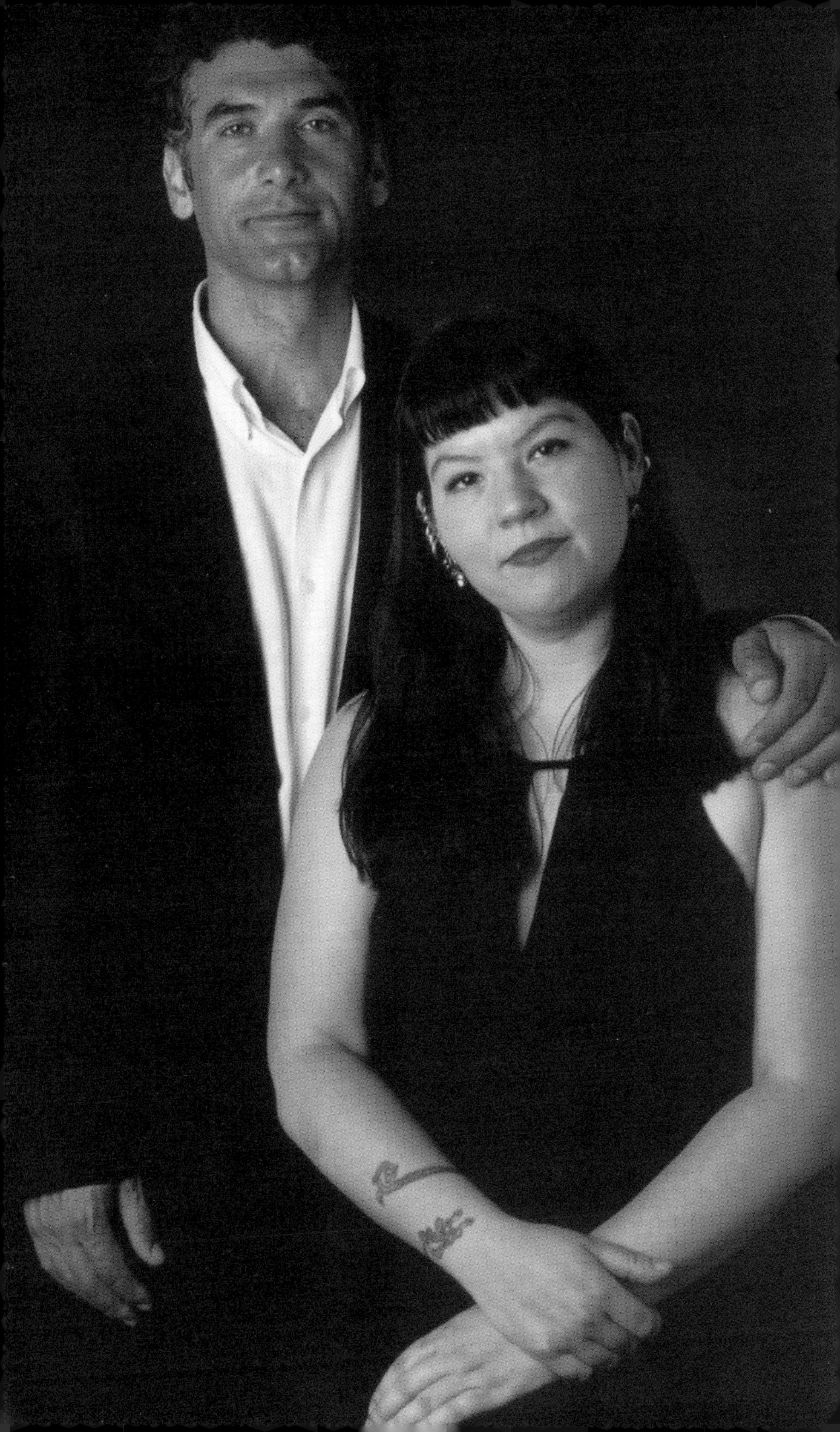

Judy Radul

The Specialists: Performing the Heterosexual Couple

SCENARIO

Although one cultural group no longer predominates among Banff's tourist population, another dominant order is exemplified by the heterosexual as the typical and primary consumer. Advertisements portray happy male-female couples in dining rooms, spas and honeymoon suites. Such images depend on the presumption that there is no alternative way of living, and they endorse one lifestyle based on a his-and-hers principle. These particular customers are depicted repeatedly in the same configuration in assorted fashions. Consumer culture thrives by maintaining this social formation, implanting it firmly into the social unconscious. Couples parade in a leisurely manner down Banff Avenue, largely unaware that they embody a specific code of behaviour. In *The Specialists*, Judy Radul worked with the notion that performance is integral to everyday assumptions.

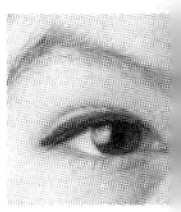

On her arrival in Banff, Judy put out a call for male actors. She interviewed and hired five men to spend time with her in public places, to fulfil an ambiguous yet over-determined role as her male companion, boyfriend, husband. She paid them to accompany her, and with a twist to the tradition of a woman with an escort, she took control of the agenda, casting each man in a different role. Judy wore the same black dress on each date—the man represented the only change in circumstance. Each couple walked along the streets of Banff, sat in the park and engaged in a variety of leisure activities. One outing included a ride on the Happy Bus from downtown to the Banff Springs Hotel, buying a purse in the shopping corridor, strolling back to town hand in hand, stopping for ice cream along the way. Banff Avenue was Judy's main stage; a commercial strip designed for shopping—it has plate-glass windows that glow with the displays of merchandise.

This private investigation was a manoeuvre from within. Judy claimed the identity of the heterosexual consumer and infiltrated the crowds. Like a double agent, she played the part with criticality and complicity. Using the spectacle as her disguise, she was the consumer and she was consumed. Judy and her date seemed like most other couples as they walked through the crowds, except that they were accompanied by a video camera. Following close behind with purpose and discretion, a videographer documented each couple's performance, recording images of the conventions of romance—kissing on the bridge, standing arm and arm beside the falls, gazing into each other's eyes over lunch. But Judy's striking urban look distinguished her visually from her sporty surroundings. She and the camera had an undeniable presence—both were equally a part of the act, highlighting the performative nature of seeing and being seen.

The Specialists appropriated a conceptual art model. Though provision was made for the characters to develop in each situation, a set of rules applied: hire five men, walk five times through town, follow your desires, record the map. Judy videotaped her investigations, capturing clichés and making notes about sexuality as a social construction.

—*Kathryn Walter*

I remember them.
I served them a sandwich, which they shared.
Yeah, they looked a little uncomfortable—like they expected Banff to be something different, something else, something other than what it was.

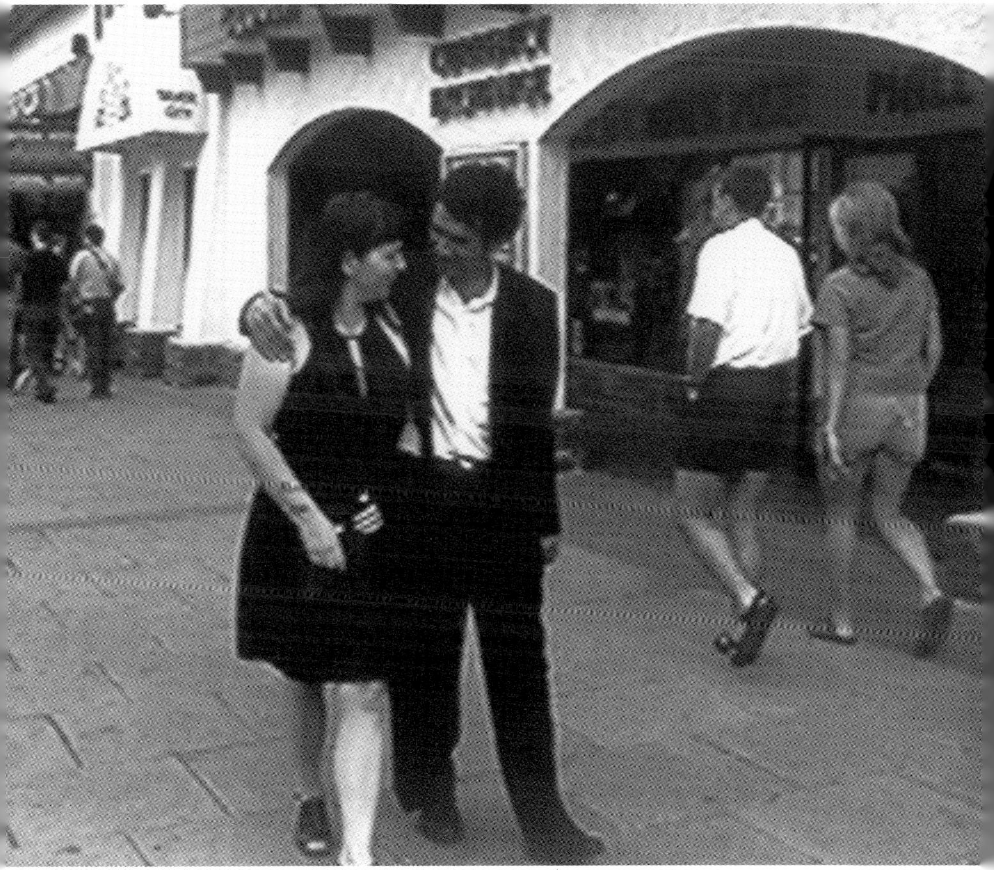

She remarked on our computerized ordering system. She seemed interested. He said it was a Texas Instrument, but it isn't.

I noticed them walking arm in arm. I liked the way that looked. We used to do the same thing. That felt good. To move through a crowd like that. The other person's body against your own. Knowing when they were going to stop or start. They were like that too.

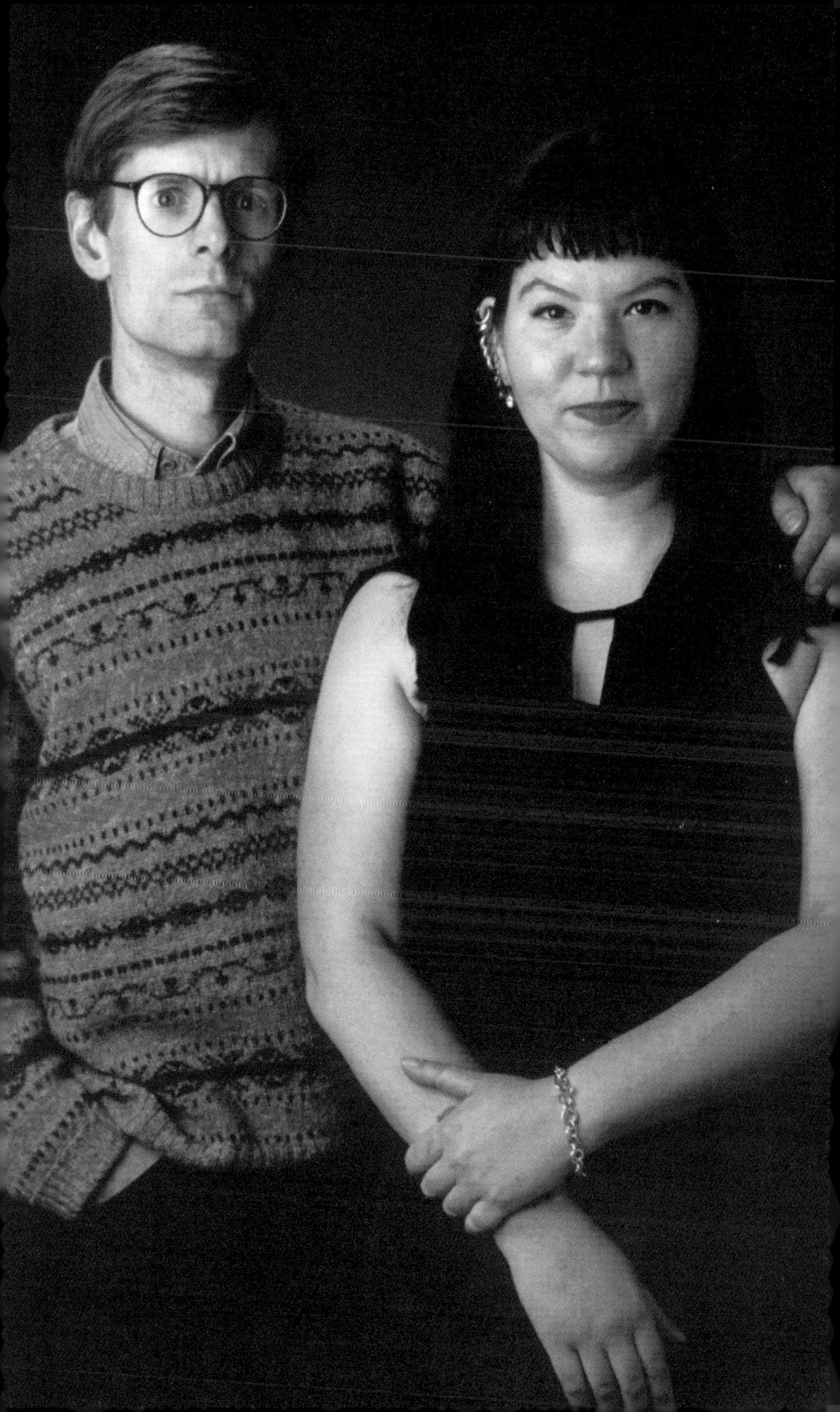

He seemed too old for her. Together they looked kind of grey. They looked like they were just going through the motions. You see a lot of that here. People thinking this beautiful scenery will be some kind of romantic backdrop, that it will make them feel in love again. But really, these mountains just remind them of what they're missing. It's too awe-inspiring. It's better for couples who are just starting out, who really are in love.

I don't remember them. We get nothing but couples in here all day long. They all look the same, as far as I'm concerned.

Oh, they were gross. Touching all the time. Feeding each other. My girlfriend and I have a name for it. PDAs. Public Displays of Affection. It's so oppressive. I can't stand watching. It's hard to avoid, though.

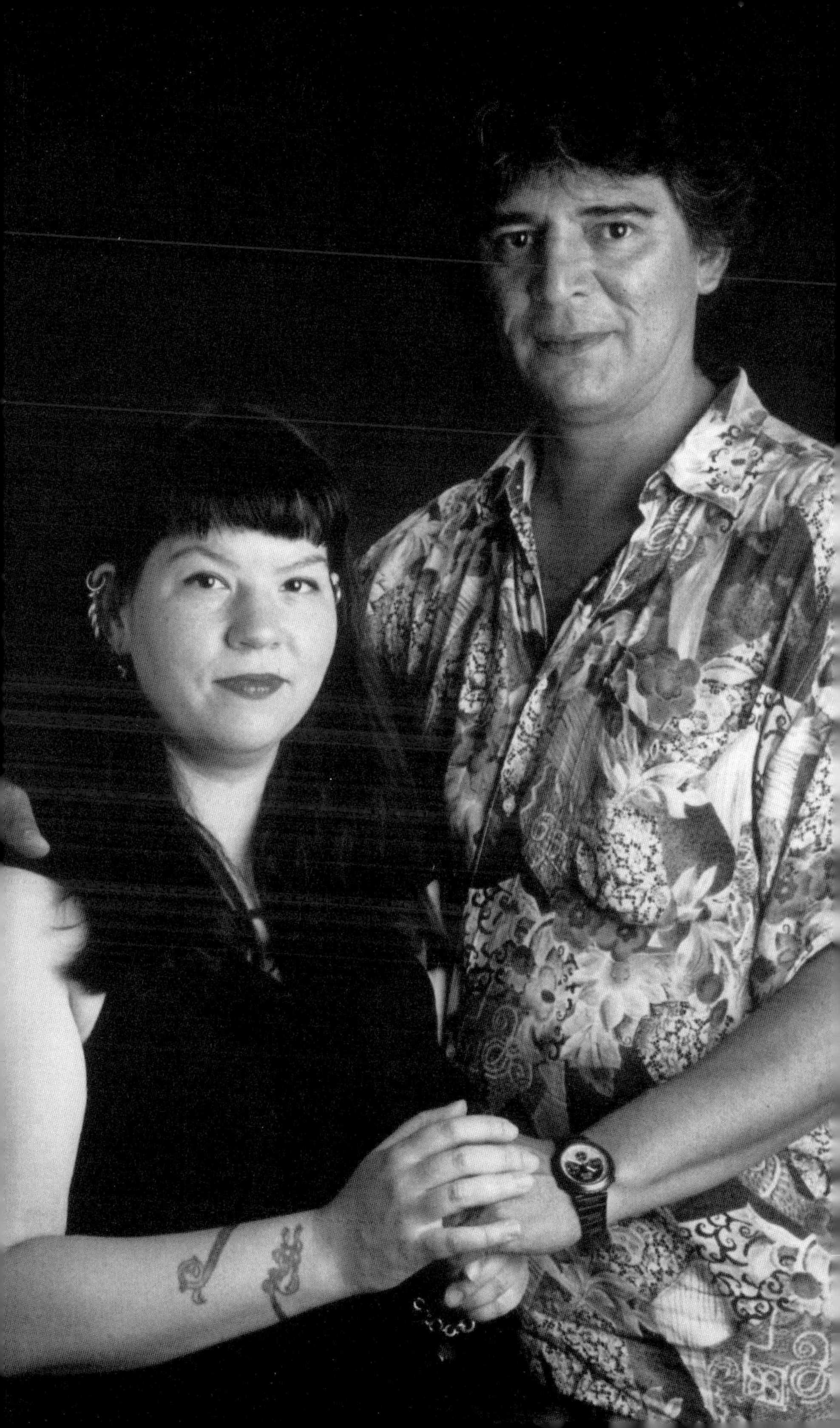

It's a way to get things done. You're out there—a bunch of little tactical units on patrol. You talk, look around, touch. Sharing the little things—ice cream, beer, observations. And everyone else is sharing them, too. Everyone else is watching you "sharing." So you have to wonder—all that sharing. But it seems to work. They could've been from here, but I doubt it.

Sometimes I wonder what kind of sex they have. Some look like it's awful, which makes me feel sick to my stomach.

I got stuck behind them in a lineup. He had his hand on the small of her back, patting it, tapping out something in time to the sound system. He said something in her ear, but she didn't respond. His hand stopped for a minute, then began again—keeping the beat.

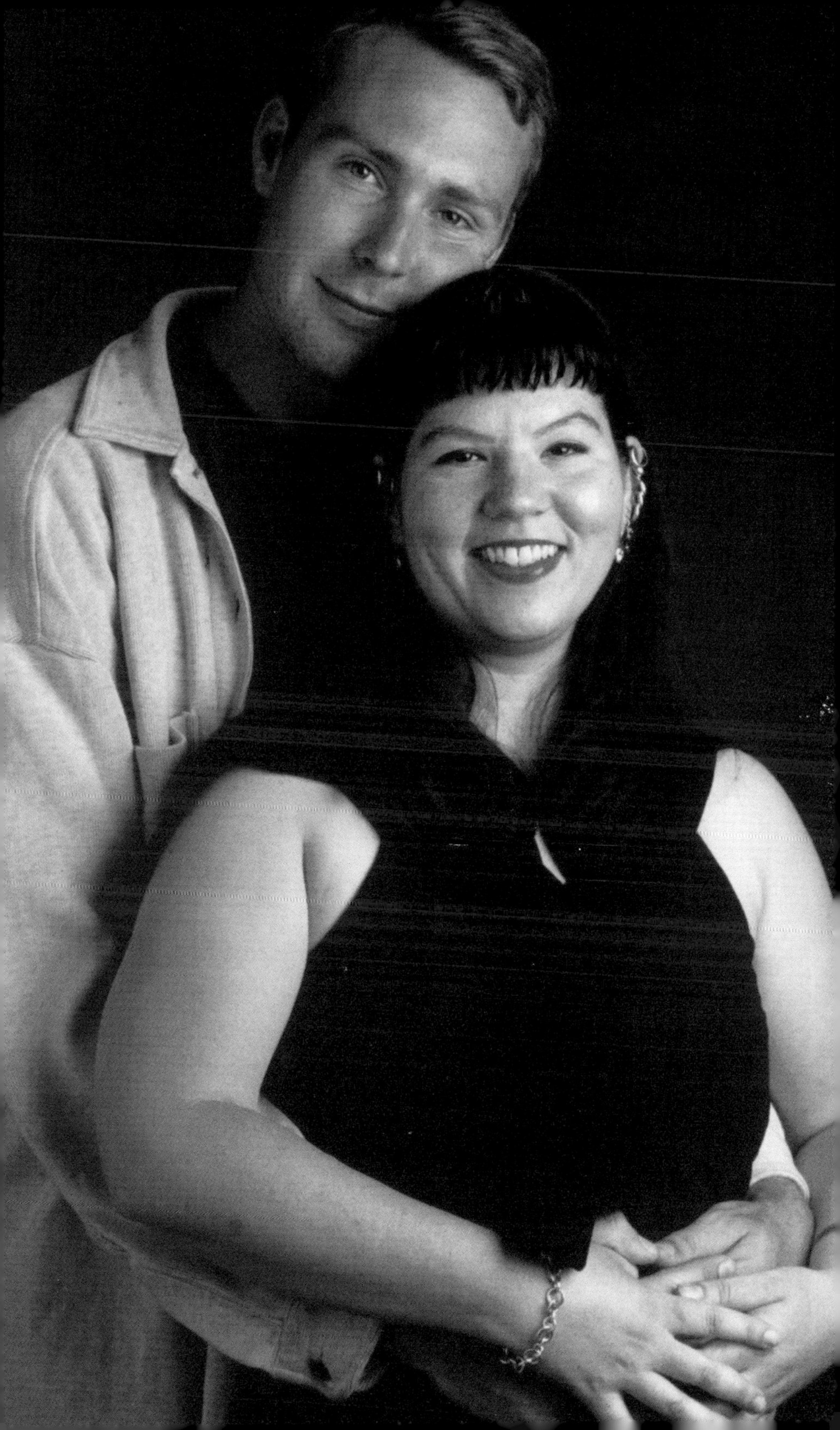

One time this guy in an Orioles cap burst in. He made a quick survey of the store. I was waiting for him to ask for help. He seemed almost distraught. A moment later a woman wearing the same kind of cap entered. Same behaviour. They saw each other, looked relieved, said nothing and quickly went back onto the street together.

They'll never remember me, but I know them. Not individually, but as a culture. A culture of couples, which I no longer fit into. They make me feel a little freakish out having coffee on my own, at my age.

She was pretty hot and so was he. I think they were into it for the short term, if you know what I mean. I could relate to that. I wouldn't have said no to a piece.

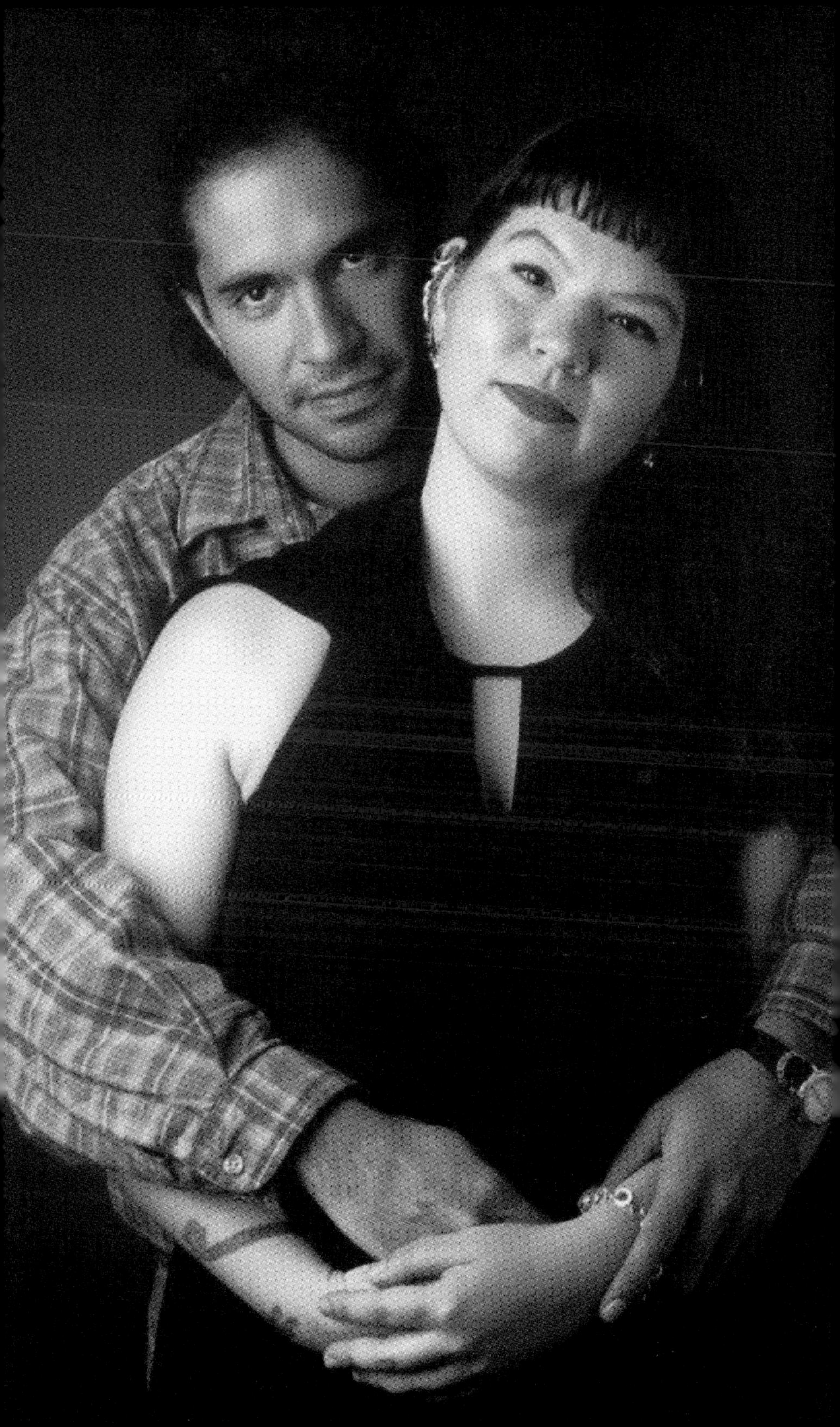

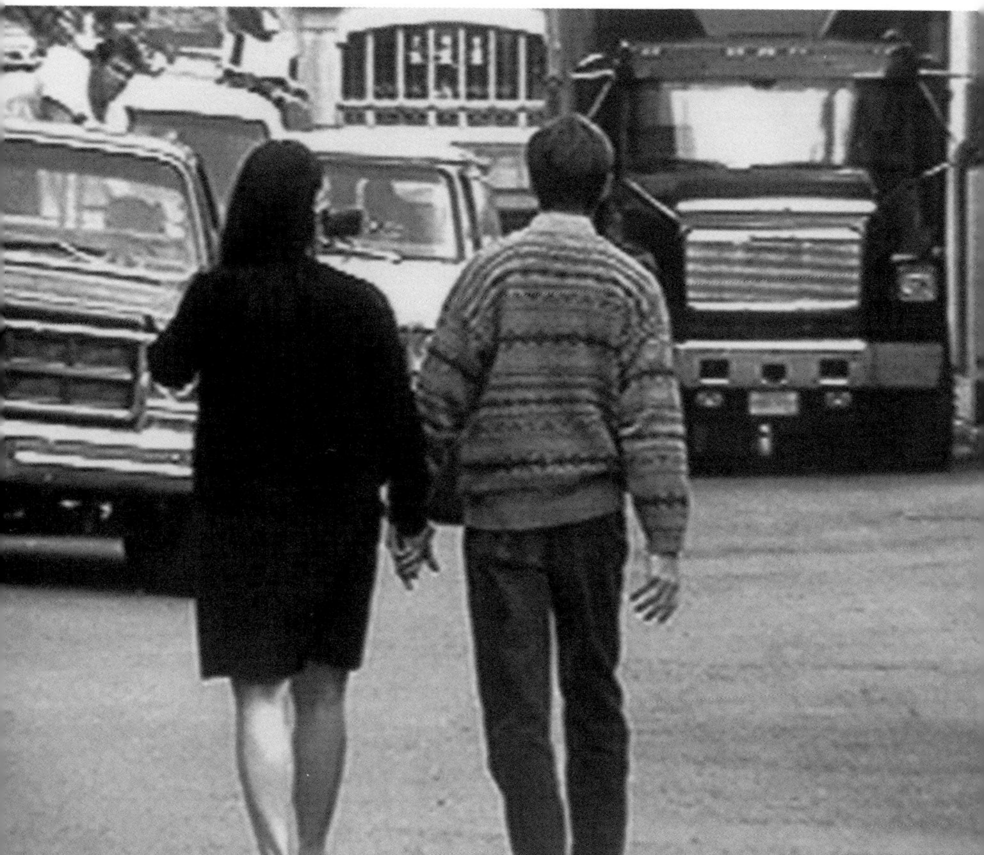

EYEWITNESS ACCOUNT

Around the Banff Centre campus, a poster announces Men Wanted. Slowly word spreads that the artist Judy Radul is recruiting five mates—of various looks, ages, types—to act as her escort. She wants to "wear" each of them for an afternoon, walk with them arm in arm and play happy couple, while she turns Banff Avenue into a theatre of erotic make-believe. Having selected her beaux, she begins the transformation. (Va-voom.) Judy-the-lover enters the scene, costumed for romance in a short black dress. She appears very urban-chic, a sexy femme fatale who baldly defies Banff's unspoken dress code of sports gear and earth tones.

Changing men as one might change outfits, Judy places herself in various heterosexual scenes of looking. Day after day, she walks the same strip of pavement, rounds the same corner, sits on the same bench, follows the same route. What interrupts the loop is our arrival as onlookers and voyeurs. Judy is a "good feminist" with a healthy appetite for documentation, and each performance is scrupulously recorded on video and in still photos. Each couple is stalked by a camera.

Judy reminds us that in the scopic space of tourism, women are both the viewers and the viewed, as much touring as toured. Women, in other words, do not circulate freely. Their travel is knotted to ethnicity, race, sexuality and class. All these factors determine which avenues are open to a woman and in what ways she will travel. The various "mates" accompanying Judy—an older white man, a young Mohawk man, et cetera—resignify her body. They change the way she inhabits the street.

Banff's streets are thus places for masquerade, where the feminine is figured only as a performance, a social charade of conjugal happiness. Judy has intensified the scopophilia inherent in tourism. At the same time, she seems to revel in the voyeuristic aspect of surveillance, appearing simultaneously as the active subject and wary object of desire.

—*Kyo Maclear*

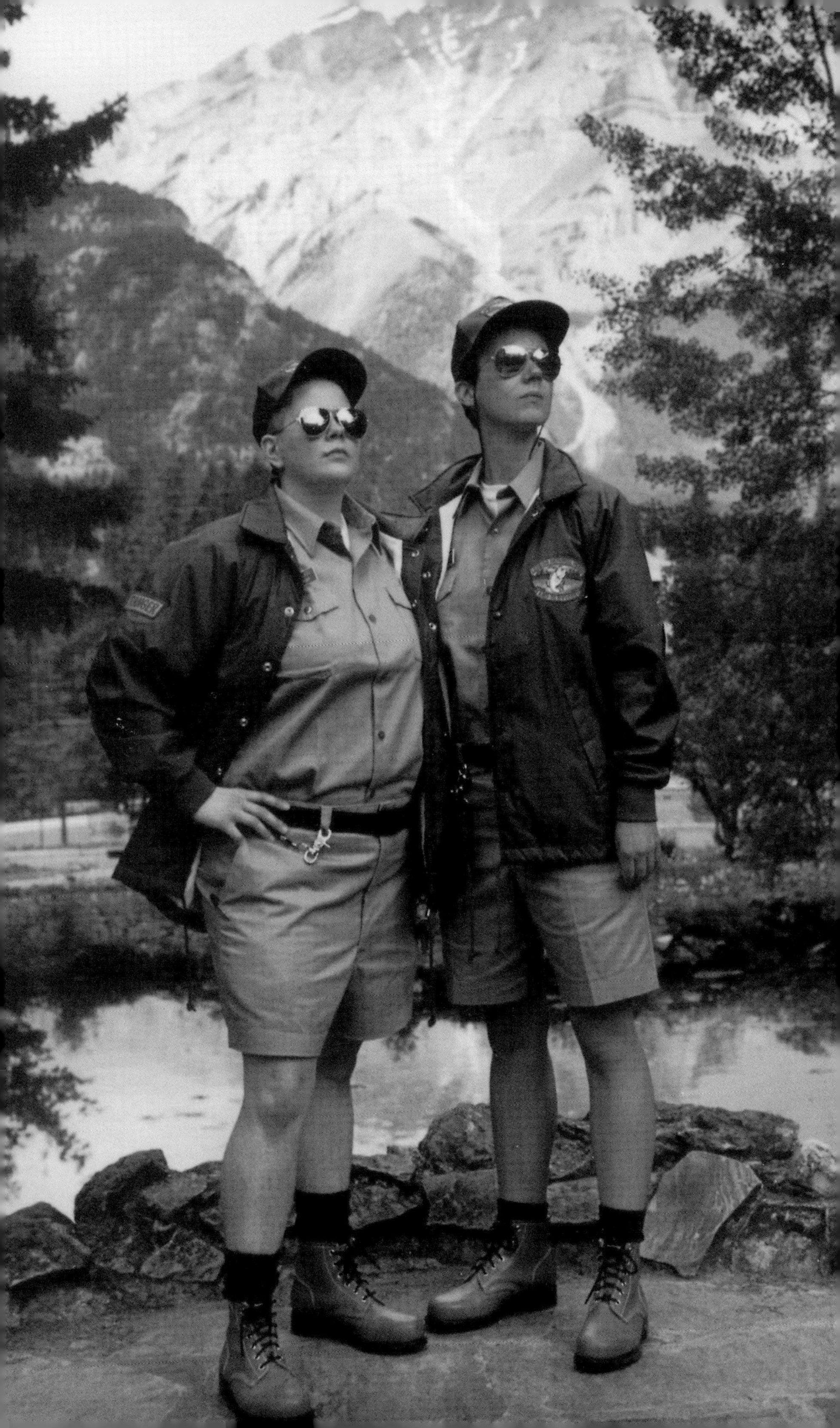

Shawna Dempsey and Lorri Millan

Lesbian National Parks & Services

SCENARIO

Shawna Dempsey and Lorri Millan arrived in Banff in their turquoise 1963 Pontiac Laurentian, dressed from head to toe in khaki gear. From their boots to their caps, they inhabited the uniforms of park rangers, complete with accessories. You could hear them coming with the jingle of their key chains, but only a close look at their badges gave away their affiliation with the Lesbian National Parks & Services. As "out" as this name may seem, in actuality it was subtly inserted into public view. The name of this organization appeared on Shawna's and Lorri's bodies with such formality and apparent legitimacy that for all intents and purposes it normalized the word *lesbian*. But it was the charm exhibited by Shawna and Lorri that gave their cause the most credibility and ultimately enabled their lesbian identities to enter a potentially threatening mainstream. The Rangers' uniforms and badges lent authority that allowed the two artists to move freely in the vast heterosexual midst, giving directions, taking photos and otherwise lending helping hands. Policies were drafted and circulated, and a recruitment day was organized in Central Park. Apart from an occasional break to do laundry, Shawna and Lorri wore their uniforms for the duration of their stay in Banff, becoming a part of the Western vernacular.

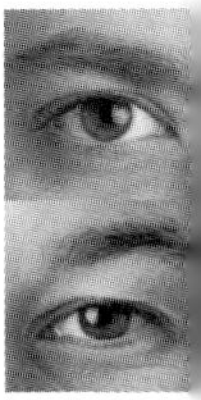

Word got around town that the Lesbian Rangers were out and about, as their brochure ended up in the hands of tourists and town residents alike, including the family of the woman portrayed on the brochure's cover. Shawna and Lorri had appropriated this photograph from a book about the Rocky Mountains published in the 1960s, and as it turned out, the woman depicted was alive and well and living on the outskirts of Banff. There was a buzz around town about this, and news got back to the Centre by word of mouth. But before any authorities were alerted or mistrust grew, the Rangers politely printed a new cover and carried on with their duties. The new brochure featured a portrait of the Rangers posing against a vista of the town. Even the administration at Banff National Park were relatively respectful, regarding the friendly impostors with more awe than suspicion. Perhaps this acceptance resulted from the Lesbian Rangers' propensity to take their own advice, watching their step, ensuring that the wilderness belongs to everyone.

Taking full responsibility for their actions, the Rangers met their audience face-to-face. Their encounters with people took place in real space, a we-are-in-this-boat-together kind of space, and in the process, a private and marginalized lifestyle was publicized; the invisible was made visible; homosexuality "came out," and a situation that was potentially contentious became matter-of-fact. Shawna and Lorri's performance was a parody, an amusing inquiry into the authority of the park ranger, but at the same time, it was a gesture of pride based on lived experience. Theirs was a play about everyday issues, and with humour in their ardent actions they engaged their audience and communicated their commitment to a way of life. There was the odd occasion of homophobic outburst, but the Rangers subdued our preconceived fears of right-wing reaction. Shawna and Lorri were truly the most endearing activists this site had ever seen.

—*Kathryn Walter*

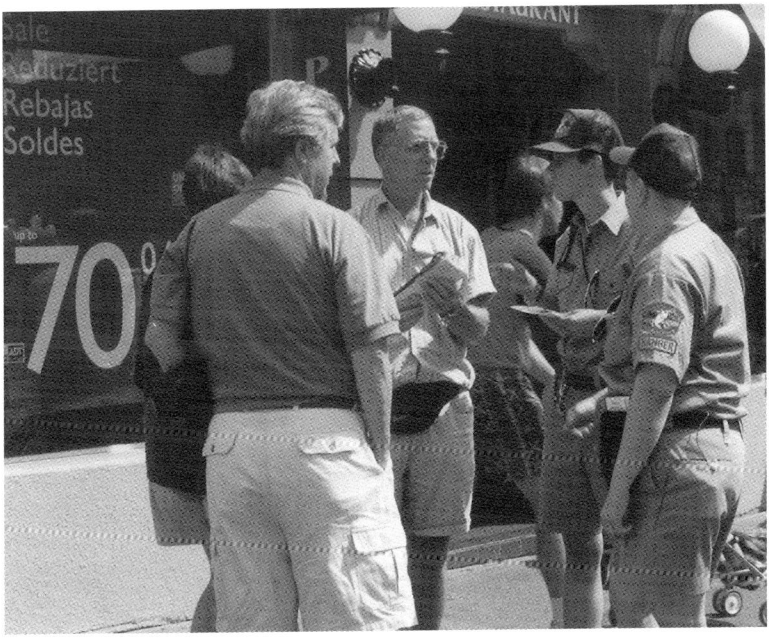
Sale
Reduziert
Rebajas
Soldes
up to
70
RANGER

LESBIAN NATIONAL PARKS & SERVICES and You!

Founded in 1997, the Lesbian Ranger Corps is a fast-growing and dynamic force of professionals dedicated to the preservation, management and proliferation of lesbian wildlife in all its forms. But we can't do it alone. There are many ways you can become involved with Lesbian National Parks & Services.

Remember, whether you live in a large urban centre or a small rural community, on a mountainside or on the vast, open prairie, Lesbian National Parks & Services depends on all citizens to create an ecosystem better suited to the diversity of lesbian wildlife just waiting to flourish. Lesbian National Parks & Services wants you! We need you. Together, we can make a difference.

Write to: **Lesbian National Parks & Services Headquarters**
485 Wardlaw Avenue, Winnipeg, MB
Canada R3L 0L9

Or e-mail: finger@escape.ca

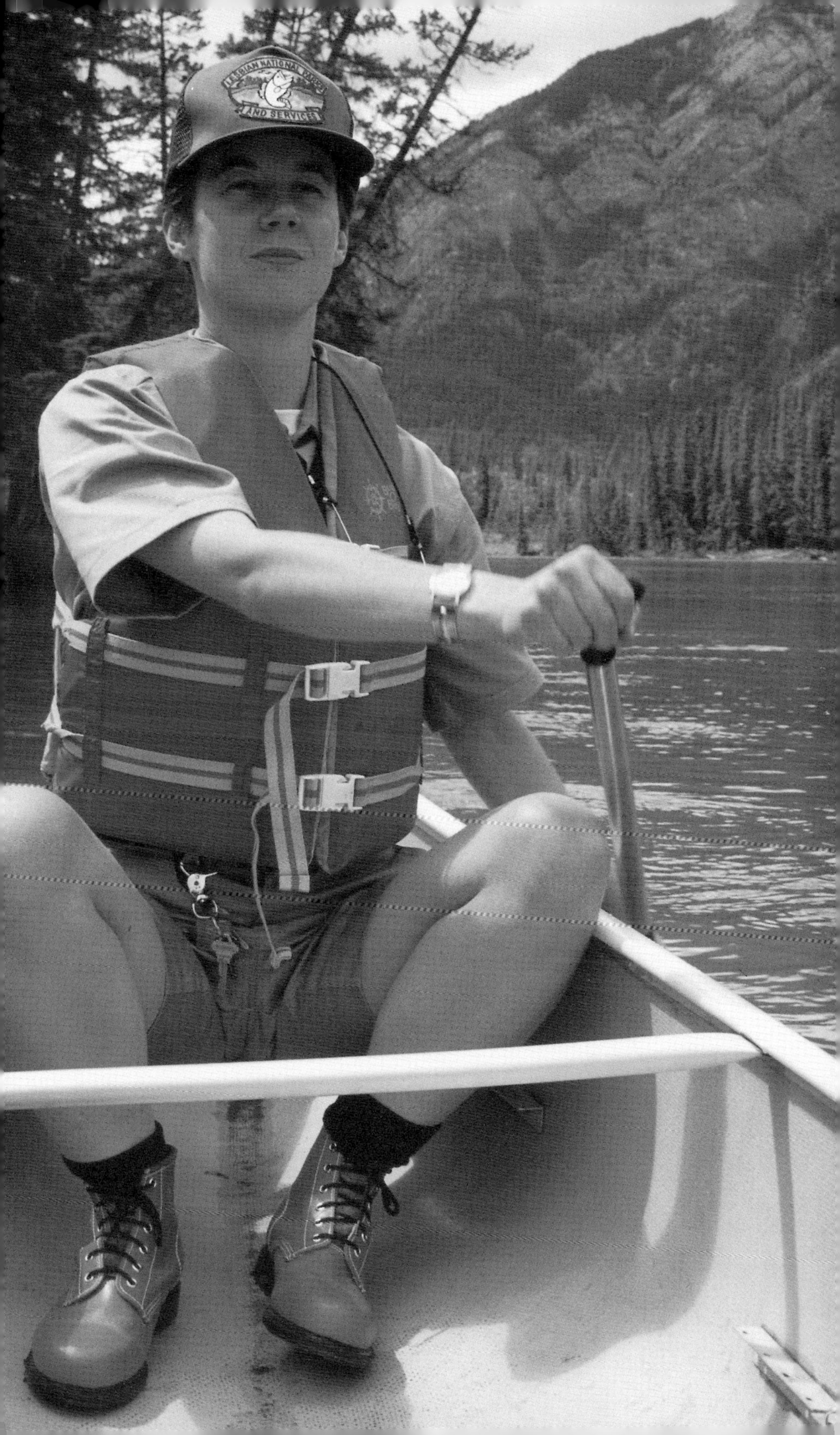
NATIONAL
AND SERVICES

LESBIAN NATIONAL PARKS & SERVICES

National Headquarters: 485 Wardlaw Avenue, Winnipeg, Manitoba Canada R3L 0L9

Ph. 204-453-8845 Fax 204-453-8845 email finger@escape.ca

Ranger Lorri Millan

FIELD REPORT NO. 13
DATE: July 10, 1997
LOCATION: Banff Avenue (southbound near Caribou Street)
TIME: 11:37

Patrolling Banff Avenue this morning, we encountered a young male *Homo sapiens*. Displaying a certain strain of XY behaviour, the male shouted, "Fucking homos," before bounding away into the throng. (We were fascinated to observe that his survival instincts were clearly intact, despite the other developmental problems he exhibited.)

Ranger Shawna Dempsey

FIELD REPORT NO. 27
DATE: July 14, 1997
LOCATION: Banff townsite
TIME: 13:00

Leading a group of potential homosexual naturalists on a brief tour of the town this afternoon, we paused to examine various sites (the invisible Lesbian Heritage House and Gardens, etc.). We were delighted that so many of the participants were seniors, proving once again that interest in the gay outdoors is not limited by age. We met at the Whyte Museum, and proceeded on a set course (highlighting various flora and fauna groups) to the Walter Phillips Gallery. The only difficulty encountered was that some of the participants insisted on referring to the trek as an "Art Walk," which we felt created doubt regarding the rigour of our scientific method. However, we, the field rangers, are confident that standards are being upheld.

Ranger Shawna Dempsey

FIELD REPORT NO. 33
DATE: July 19, 1997
LOCATION: The Banff Centre for the Arts
TIME: Various

Many residents at The Banff Centre for the Arts consistently exhibit "Ranger Envy." This is evident in their behaviour, including (but not limited to) attempting to buy the world-famous green-and-tan uniform, and when thwarted, asking to "try on" various parts of the regulation gear and then cleverly "forgetting" to return them.

Ranger Lorri Millan

FIELD REPORT NO. 47
DATE: July 21, 1997
LOCATION: Campsite, Two Jack Lake
TIME: 21:47

Patrolling the campsite, Ranger Dempsey and I sighted a pair of bewildered short-haired females. Clothed in colourful cotton, they carried the clear markings of the not-uncommon "Helper" lesbian. Because they displayed signs of confusion and fatigue, we approached cautiously. After contact was established, we ascertained that they were suffering from disorientation as a result of being separated from their urban pack, or "community." Casual contact with the Lesbian Rangers seemed to allay their fears, acting as a stopgap until they could migrate home.

LESBIAN NATIONAL PARKS & SERVICES

National Headquarters: 485 Wardlaw Avenue, Winnipeg, Manitoba Canada R3L 0L9

Ph. 204-453-8845 Fax 204-453-8845 email finger@escape.ca

Ranger Shawna Dempsey

FIELD REPORT NO. 56
DATE: July 24, 1997
LOCATION: Central Park
TIME: 15:00

Today's recruitment drive was very successful. The colourful "Lesbian National Parks and Services WANT YOU!" banner and the pink lemonade attracted countless passersby, who were most interested in the service and how they might become involved. Among our more animated guests was a day camp of thirsty children who were very excited by our Junior Ranger programs. (On a personal note, I must say it is extremely satisfying to have eager young faces look up at our crisply uniformed selves with naked awe and respect.)

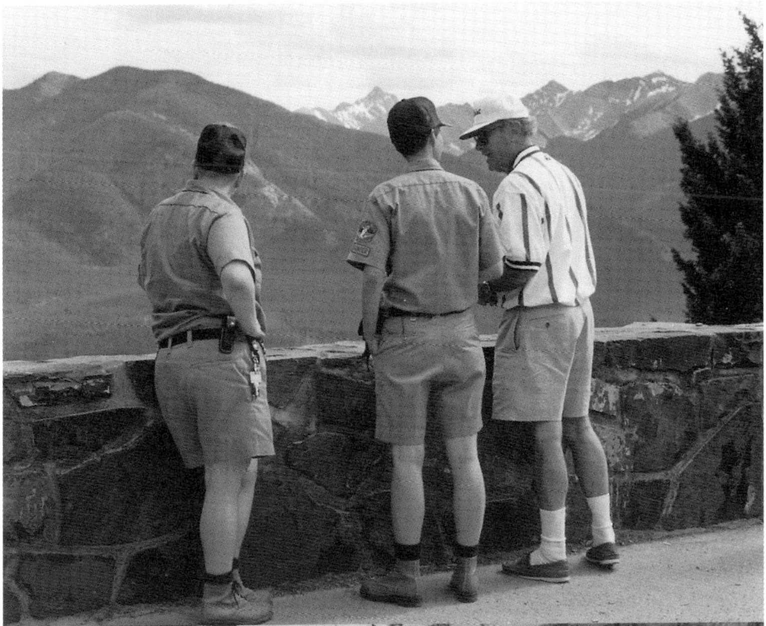

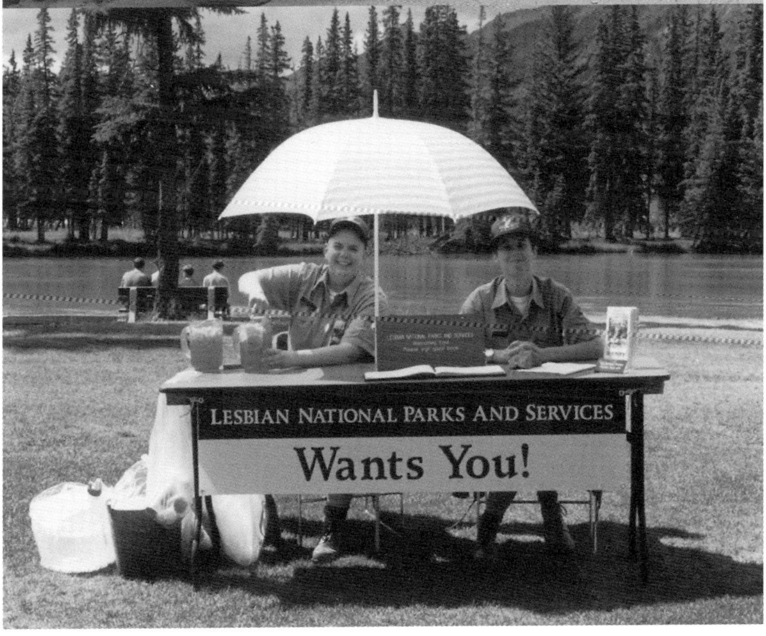
LESBIAN NATIONAL PARKS AND SERVICES
Wants You!

LESBIAN NATIONAL PARKS & SERVICES

National Headquarters: 485 Wardlaw Avenue, Winnipeg, Manitoba Canada R3L 0L9

Ph. 204-453-8845 Fax 204-453-8845 email finger@escape.ca

Rangers Shauna Dempsey and Lorri Millan

FINAL REPORT
DATE: August 1, 1997

BACKGROUND:
The first field study of the recently formed Lesbian National Parks & Services was conducted in Banff for a period of nineteen days, July 7–25 inclusive. Banff was chosen because of its wealth of natural habitat, dearth of lesbian plant and wildlife and a largely tourist human population who display some interest in the environment, and were therefore seen as potentially impressionable/educatable/vulnerable to LNPS.

GOALS:
Rangers Dempsey and Millan sought to:
– promote the introduction of gay and lesbian flora and fauna into the Banff area
– identify and nurture the small existing feral homosexual population
– educate regarding the importance of lesbian wildlife in any healthy environment

METHODOLOGY:
Week 1 – needs assessment and general survey of the area
Week 2 – implementation of homosexual agenda
Week 3 – recruitment

FINDINGS:

The lack of openly lesbian populations of any species was even more marked than initially feared. However, the Banff area itself is distinguished by an ethic of "unlimited growth," as evidenced by the exponential increase in tourism (four million visitors annually in 1997, which is expected to double in the next decade). After much careful study, we concluded that it seems possible that within this framework the introduction of homosexual species indigenous to the area might also lead to exponential multiplication, transforming the gay-wasteland-that-is-Banff into a virtual Galapagos of homosexual wildlife.

CONCLUSION:

Despite the challenges encountered by our first field team, the Rangers succeeded in establishing a beachhead in the heterosexual wilderness. We feel that the team's approach (exploiting rampant consumerism as a model by which to achieve explosive homo growth) will be studied for years to come and can be used to help form new and even more effective strategies for the furthering of Lesbian National Parks & Services' ambitions. We see a strong possibility for a more out and positive future, but it is crucial that our work (introduction, protection, preservation, advocacy) in the Banff area continue. Furthermore, we are confident that the Lesbian Rangers, armed with their experiences in Banff National Park, are now ready to proceed to other ecosystems throughout the country.

EYEWITNESS ACCOUNT

Visitors have started carrying around Lesbian Park Rangers pamphlets as conversation pieces. (I've noticed more than a few Banff Centre residents with conspicuously stuffed jacket pockets.) The pamphlet, an official-looking guide, replete with references to mythical lesbian landmarks, appropriates the bizarre idioms of Tourist Board copy to insinuate other routes into Banff's social and historical wilderness. The ecological views of Lorri and Shawna garner such warm and wide reception that it would seem that lesbians can finally come out of the woods of obscurity.

The Lesbian Park Rangers, unlike the Mounties co-opted by Disney, can be touted as 100 per cent Canadian. Lorri with her Erik Estrada glasses and Shawna with her Ranger hat periodically tipped to passersby both appear well scrubbed and approachable. In fact, they are strikingly less officious than their "real-life" counterparts. Their witty banter and deadpan delivery have made them favourites on the Banff Centre campus and in town.

It is amazing, but I have yet to see them out of uniform or off duty. The tone of their performance has been sustained, their personae have been played "straight," so to speak, for three whole weeks. Gradually the surrogate rangers are becoming ever more real, ever more familiar. Of course, there are repeated references to "the funny lesbians in costume," but the conceptual satire seems to have titillated visitors (myself included) to the point that we have become willing participants in the masquerade. Are we falling prey to parody? Or is the fiction unravelling the real, its centre and margins?

This would be side-show entertainment were it not for the highly suggestive and involving nature of the performance. The Rangers' starched uniforms and earnest demeanour have encouraged a Pavlovian response—visitors all seeming to cry, "Lead me!" At a certain level I can understand the reaction, having been semiologically trained during a fourth-grade trip to Algonquin Park to see rangers as "my friends." Less immediately obvious, however, are the broader implications of the masquerade.

Lorri and Shawna, you see, have fused stereotypes to create a new social breed. The first thing they want us to know is that nothing is what it seems: not the mythical "lesbian" (demonized as a social threat, target and outsider), or the equally fictionalized "ranger" (celebrated as a front-line guardian of the Canadian wilderness). The Lesbian Park Rangers make it clear that social scripts, determining who will be loved, hated and revered, can be easily scrambled. Identities can be cross-wired and reprogrammed because they are based on unstable attributes.

Thus, Lorri and Shawna test social definitions and values. They know it is difficult to vilify someone who is there to protect and guide you (hence homophobes, who are so insanely resistant to seeing gays and lesbians in care-giving professions), and even harder when that someone bears a striking resemblance to an erstwhile Canadian folk hero.

—*Kyo Maclear*

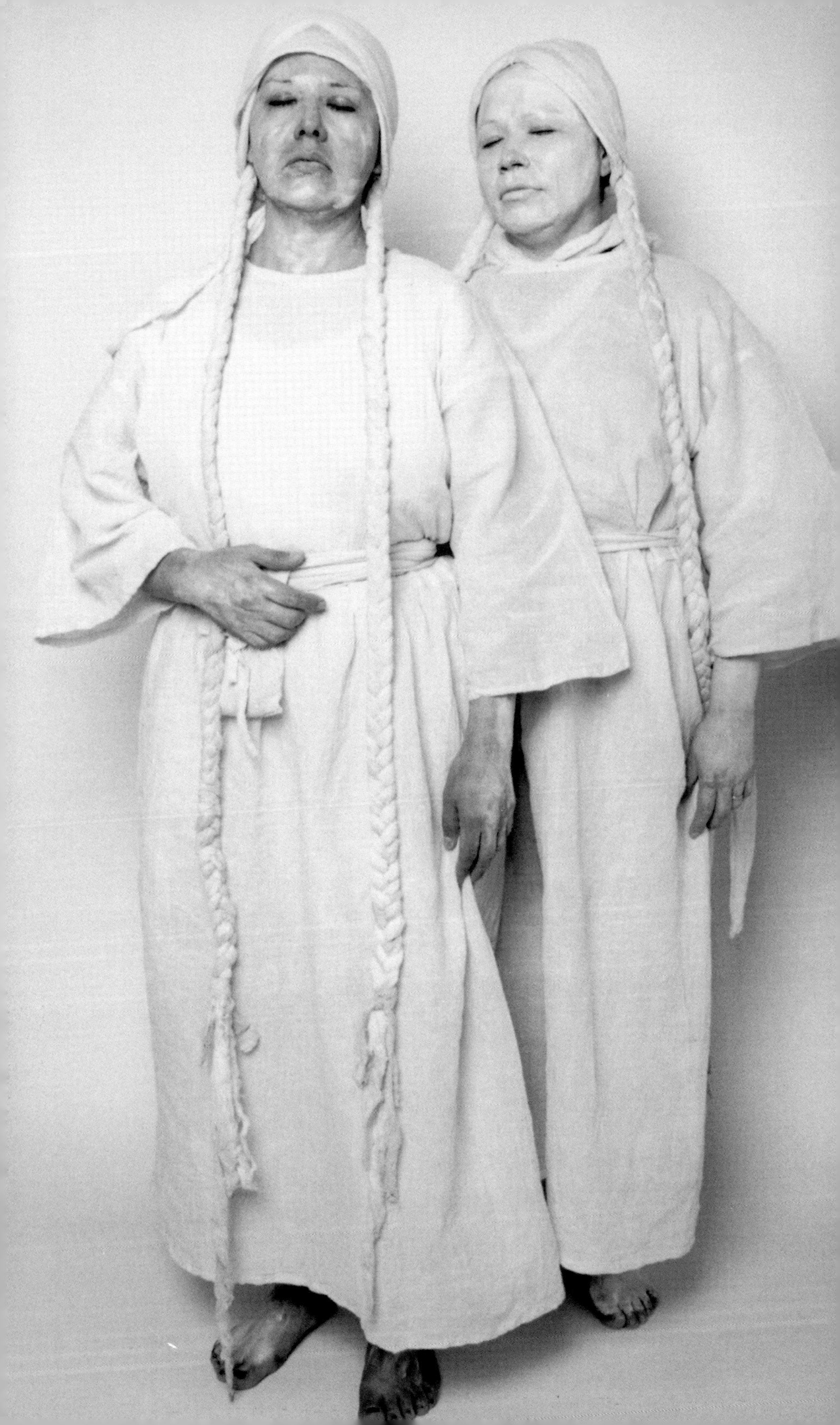

Old Sister/New Sister

SCENARIO

The presence of First Nations people in Banff has been relegated to references to the past and represented by an array of mass-produced dolls in kitschy regalia. These petty mementos are simple reminders of a complex history that has left the first peoples of this area with a persistent struggle for physical and cultural survival. Signage trivializes Aboriginal culture in every corner of this commodified landscape, from Totem Souvenirs to the Sundance Mall. Shelley Niro and Faye HeavyShield were among few Aboriginal people present in Banff's contemporary populace, and yet a chief's head cast in concrete, on the main street bridge, symbolically presides over the river below. In their project, *Old Sister/New Sister*, Shelley and Faye addressed this schism between past and present, presence and absence.

Faye arrived in Banff from Calgary, to join Shelley who arrived from her home in Brantford, Six Nations. They had discussed ideas for a site intervention in preceding months, but only by phone and the occasional letter, so their project took shape in the first few days of meeting at Banff. The form of a braid was principal to their concept, and the weaving of both material and conceptual layers was essential to their collaboration. Linking two Aboriginal perspectives and contemporary culture with spiritual tradition made their private investigation a personal exploration. For *Old Sister/New Sister*, Shelley and Faye designed costumes adapted from an Aboriginal ancestral dress, using white linen dyed in tea. The material was cut and sewn into garments and long braided wigs to create a ghostlike guise from the past.

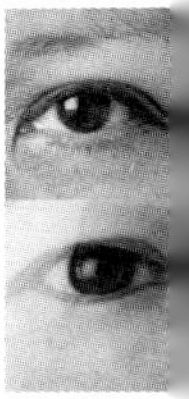

The artists scouted locations around Banff, finding a flat piece of land that juts into the river downstream from Bow Falls, where the water makes a fork in the surrounding landscape. One morning, with suitcases packed full of costumes and props, they claimed this bit of turf as their own. The site itself was a natural stage, a part of the land with just enough distinction to suggest a site of ritual. Here, they unpacked their gear, starting with a sheet of thin, transparent plastic with which they constructed a modest shelter by binding the four corners between two trees. In front of this screen, they laid a large red-ochre-stained cloth that Faye had made from contemporary children's clothes stitched together in the form of a circle. Then they began their performance, which would last through the morning. With their costumes, makeup and a mirror each, they sat on this spot, transforming themselves with white garments, white wigs and white body paint, assisting each other in preparing their attire, passing the time in an earnest but unhurried fashion.

Shelley and Faye attracted the attention of droves of tourists who arrived in vans and buses at Bow Falls. Many thought the artists were odd, assuming they were members of a strange religious sect. Others hung around, perchance to catch a glimpse of a television producer. Questions, presumptions and speculations buzzed among the onlookers, while Shelley and Faye exchanged whispers and giggles, holding their ground in a mysterious yet determined manner. After about an hour of completing their ensembles, collecting stones and observing the observers, the artists moved to the transparent screen and sliced it down the middle, making an incision through which they could walk. They retrieved the remaining contents of their suitcases, passing the goods through this slit in the screen. A coffee urn and cups, a Walkman, the day's newspaper, sunglasses and two cans of Coke accumulated on the red-ochre cloth, and Shelley and Faye spent the rest of the morning having breakfast and reading the news. People circulated, many looking for an explanation for this activity, but the artists stayed in place, keeping the audience at bay, while our cameras both objectified and protected them. Documenting this piece was a conspicuous act, but we tried to minimize the intrusion so that the performance could retain its quality of private ritual.

It was apparent that site-seeing is attended by certain assumptions, and Shelley and Faye were undoubtedly out of place in the popular eye. They were able to claim their site with no disruptions, but their unusual attire gave them an ominous appearance. Around noon, they got up, packed their bags and returned to the safer context of the Banff Centre. In the shelter of the gallery they continued their project. Here they put their costumes on display and spent sessions in the gallery adding materials and objects to their braided wigs. They gathered natural fibres and found objects, weaving sticks, ballpoint pens and miscellaneous items into their wigs. The white linen turned into blue denim, winding through time and space as the braid grew in length across the floor.

—*Kathryn Walter*

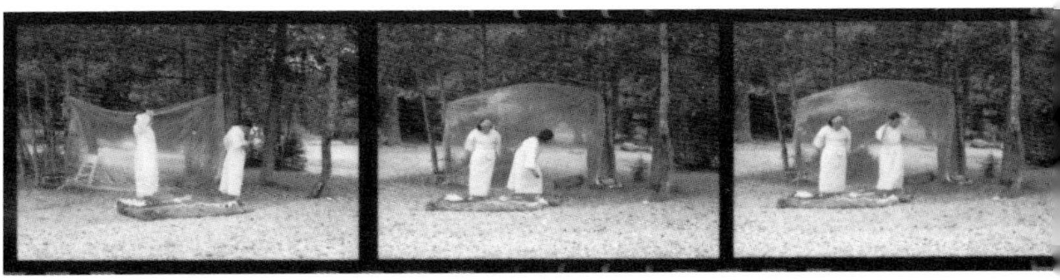

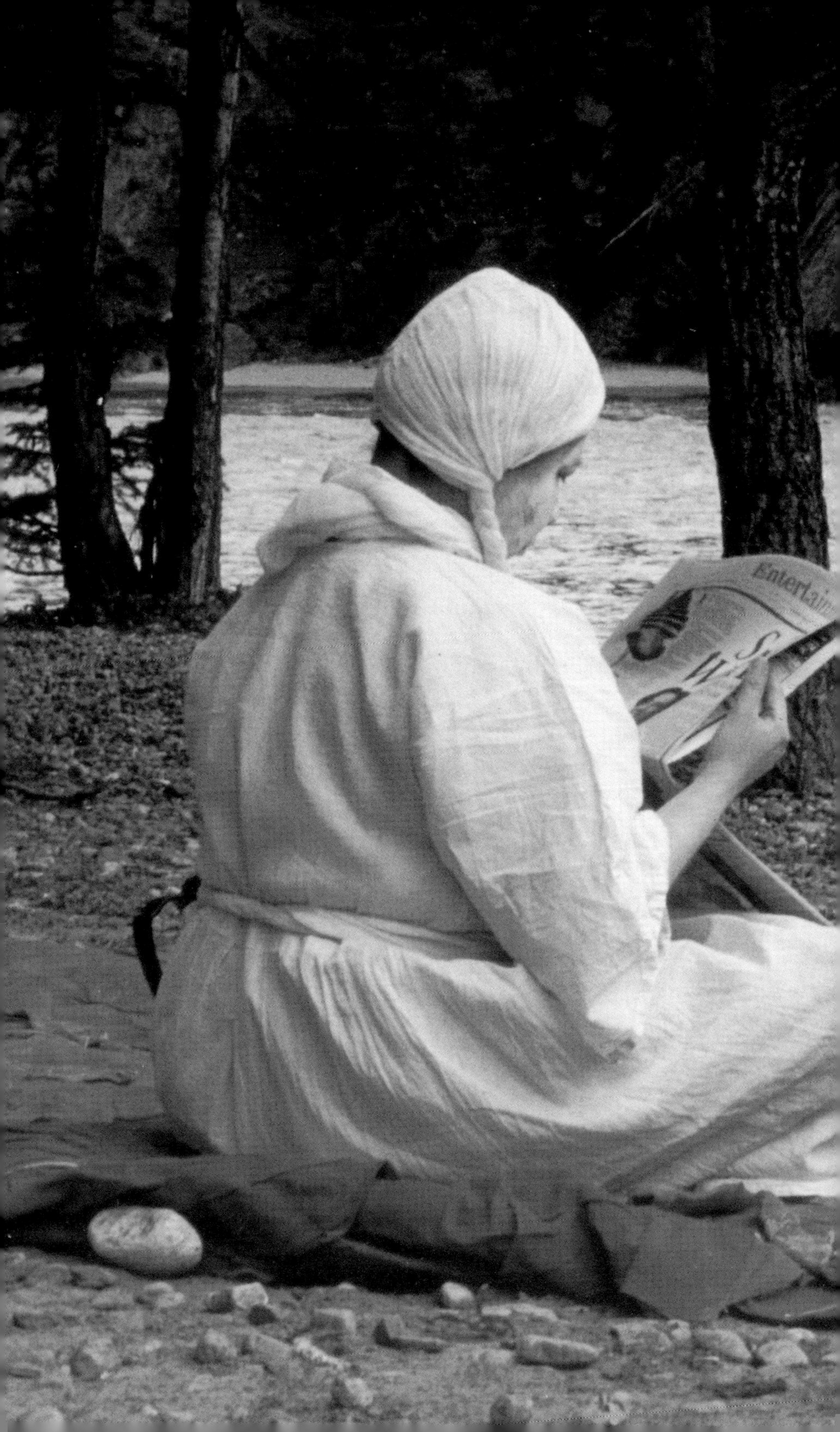

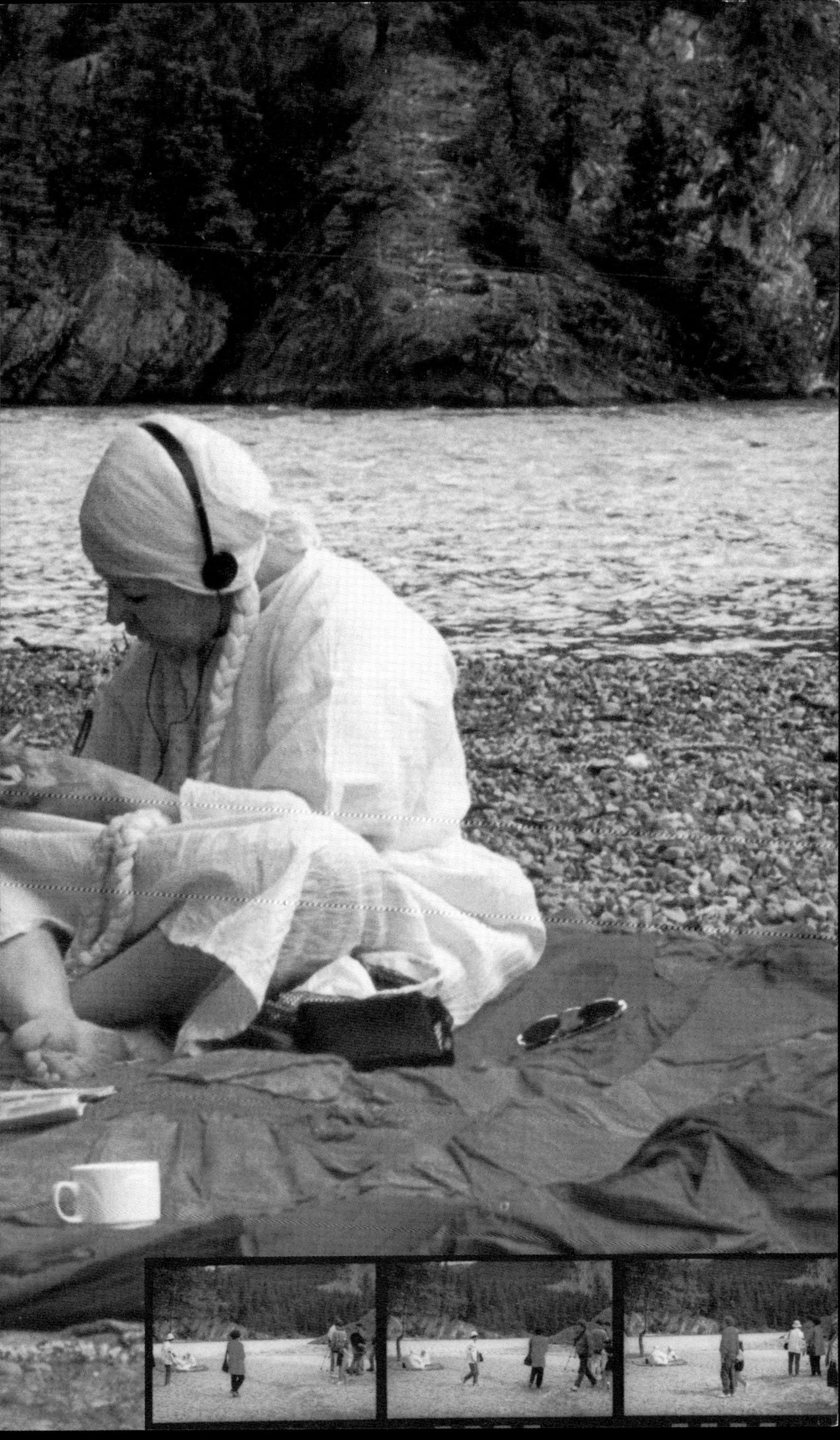

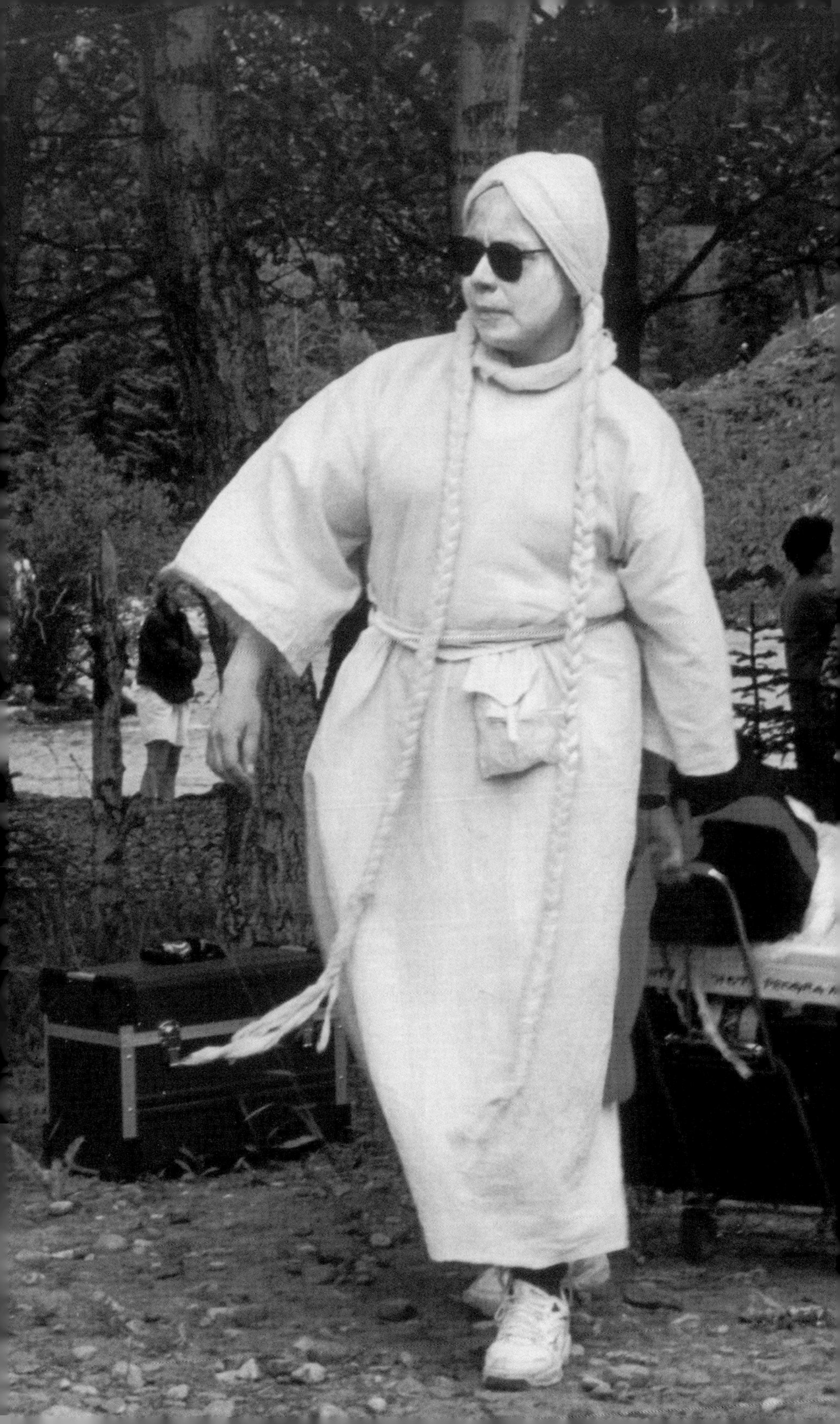

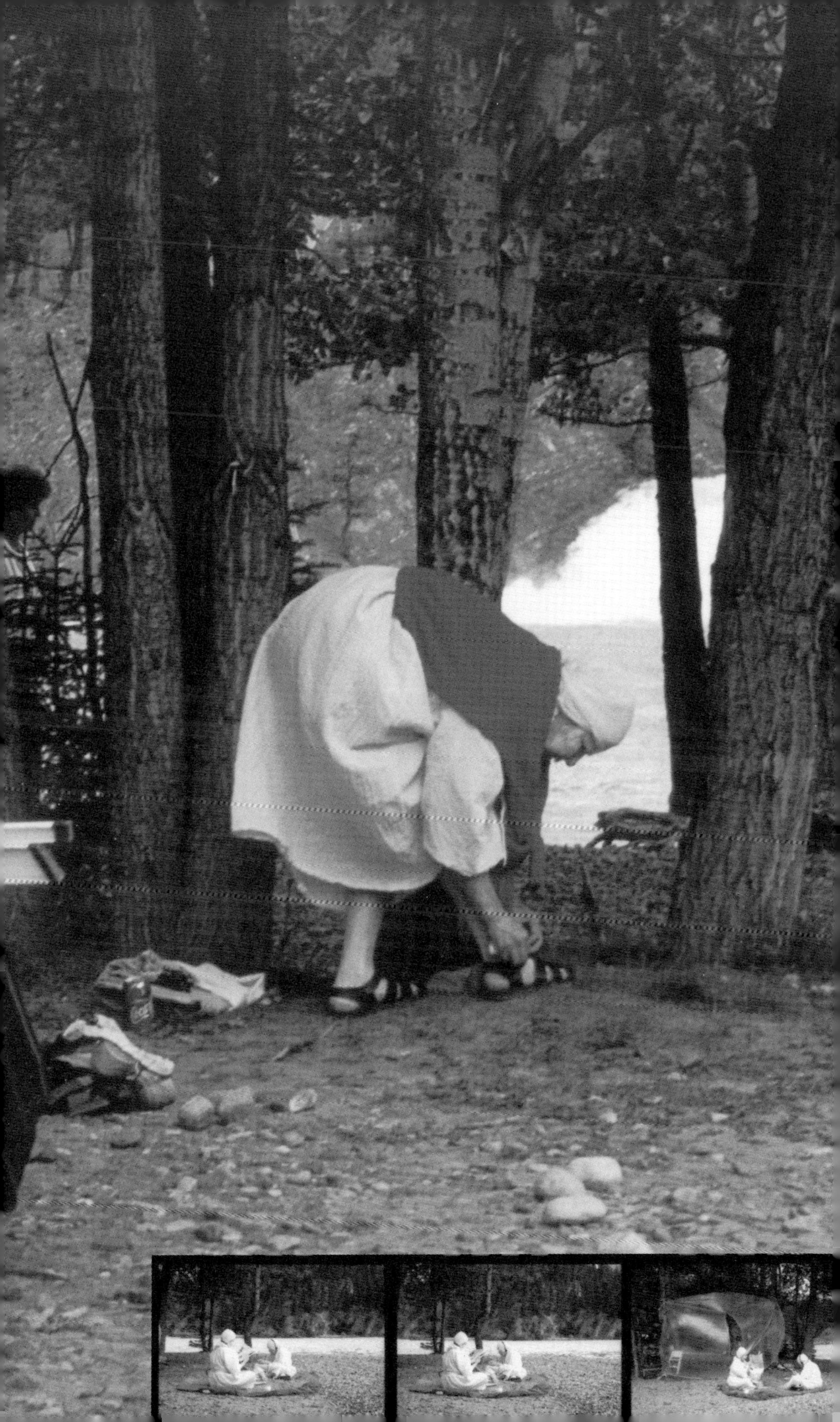

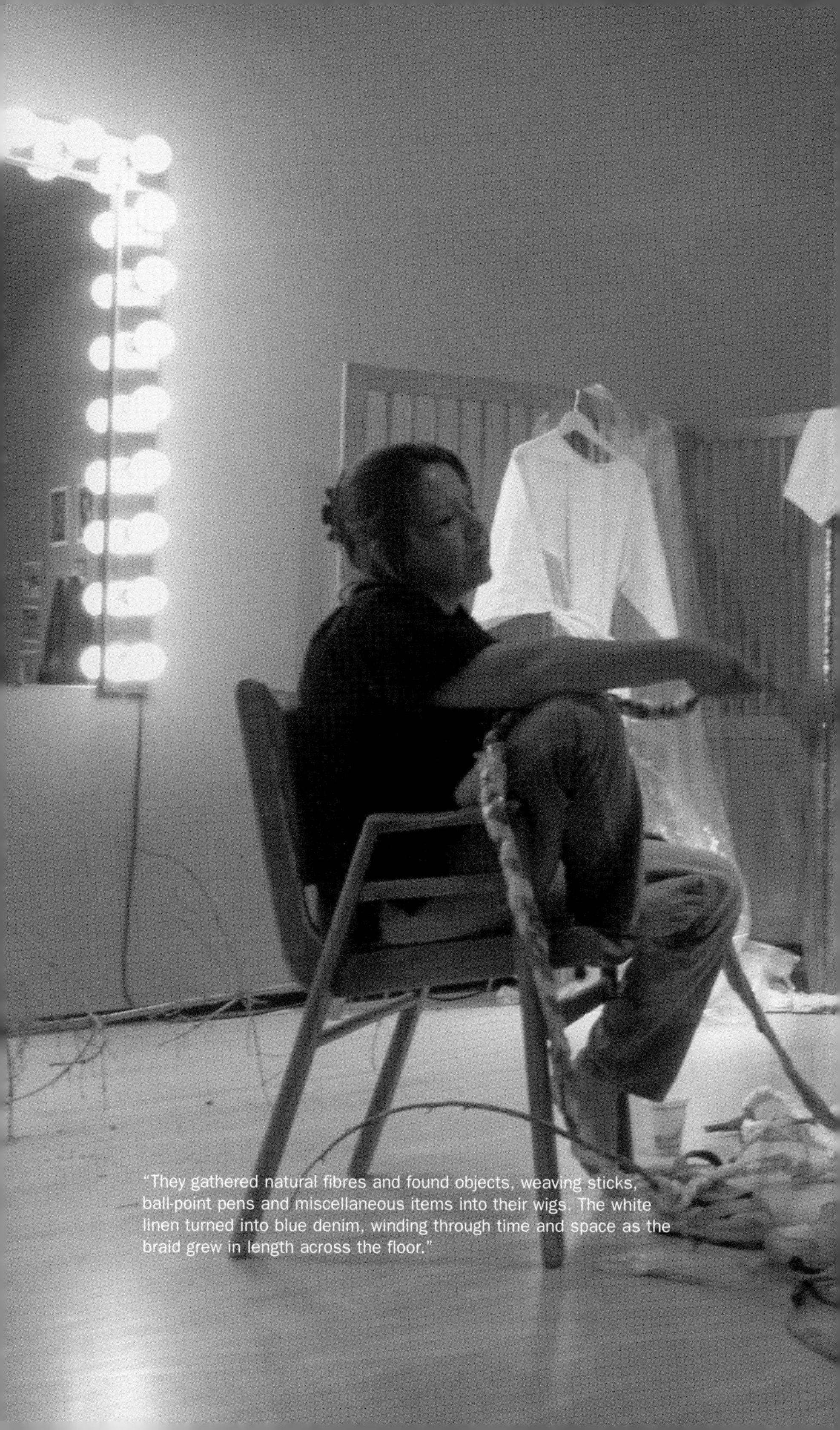

"They gathered natural fibres and found objects, weaving sticks, ball-point pens and miscellaneous items into their wigs. The white linen turned into blue denim, winding through time and space as the braid grew in length across the floor."

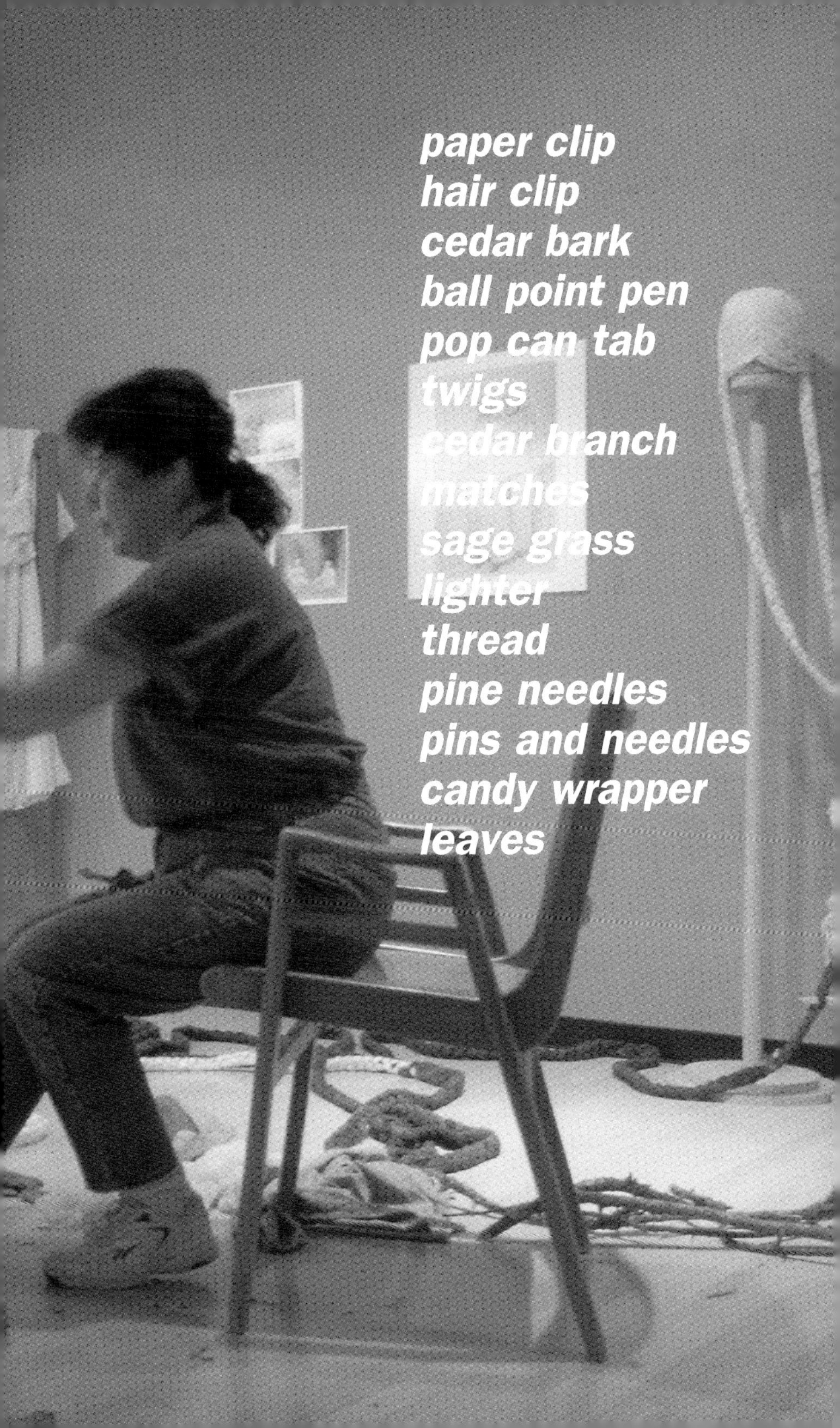
paper clip
hair clip
cedar bark
ball point pen
pop can tab
twigs
cedar branch
matches
sage grass
lighter
thread
pine needles
pins and needles
candy wrapper
leaves

EYEWITNESS ACCOUNT

If one explores the image of the Aboriginal peoples in dominant discourse, one usually finds that it tends not to be associated with anyone or anything living. Instead, Aboriginal histories are plopped in the aspic of Canadian heritage, stuck in a permanent past tense. In tourist literature, the "native" is unrelated to contemporary life, sometimes seen as local exoticism, generally excised from the mainstream.

Faye HeavyShield and Shelley Niro have stepped into the fray to reanimate the connections between the past and the present. They have made a performance of time travel, seating themselves on a red cloth in the woods, faces caked with white powder, bodies draped in white "ancestral" robes. They have wandered off the beaten track to enter into deserted places of memory. In so doing, they occupy the so-called empty and untamed wilderness, invoking the spirit of indigenous peoples who inhabited the area for centuries.

Despite a history of heavy surveillance in the area around Banff—the mapping activities of early explorers and naturalists, the establishment of the RCMP and regulated nature reserves—Faye and Shelley remind us that some experiences have not been telescoped into view. Their predecessors witnessed the ravages of development, and they are here to bear witness to the inequities of power that continue today.

The performance takes place amid some trees at the foot of Bow Falls. It consists of mundane activity that juxtaposes articles of communal life and mementos of an existence in harmony with nature with items from the commodified present. Land-forms and all things "green" are part of the environment, but so too are such objects as a coffee pot, a Coke can and a *Calgary Herald*. Their sense of the world is unsentimental but still haunted by the past.

The white powder masks and the flowing costumes act as shields to keep tourists at a distance. Theirs is an anti-performance. (When one happens upon a self-contained activity, one is an intruder.) It is also "unphotogenic," as Faye and Shelley refuse to provide a "good shot" of Aboriginal life. They offer the roving tourist nothing that can be appropriated. Instead, their quiet performance challenges our Etch-A-Sketch view of the land and its resources, whereupon we clear space, swipe the screen, so that a new drama can be enacted. The artists show us that history is as thick as peat moss. Keeping a vigil in the dappled sunlight, two women bearing the grit of the wind, they compose a ritual to symbolize the traditional and spiritual connections that colonialism and tourism have not been able to suppress.

—*Kyo Maclear*

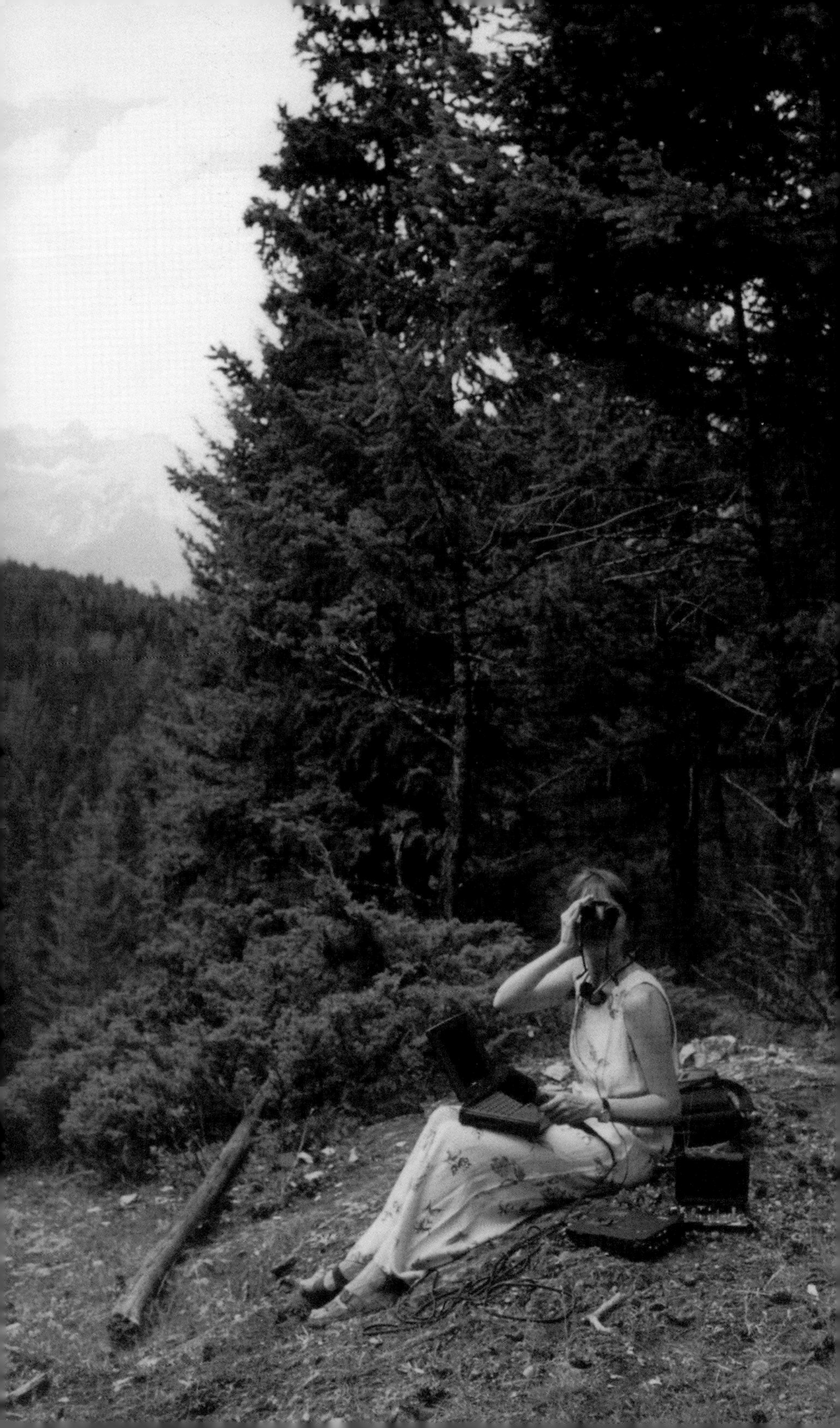

Kathy Kennedy

Paradio

SCENARIO

Banff Avenue is where the town's resident and tourist communities merge. It is a route that some take to work or to buy groceries and sundry items, but principally it is a place where people shop for pleasure rather than by necessity. The street has a commercial flow uninterrupted by buskers or panhandlers or people on strike—no rallies or riots or social unrest. Though this strip has been host to a variety of festivals and parades, it had not seen the like of Kathy Kennedy's *Paradio*, a procession of a rather unusual sort.

Kathy came to town with boxes and bundles of electronic devices, equipment to compose musical arrangements and radio transmissions. She found allies among the Banff Centre's visual artists, musicians and writers, and led sixteen such residents in a "sonic parade" down Banff Avenue, gathering wayward souls along the way. The procession began at one end of the strip and proceeded along the sidewalk for several blocks, through throngs of pedestrian traffic on a busy afternoon. This eclectic parade had no floats, marching bands or baton twirlers; rather, it was a chorus of tones and rhythms that mixed with the sounds of the street. A wooden pole bound by an electric wire was held by the leader, serving both as ornament and antenna, connecting portable radios carried by the chanting participants. This performance claimed public space through the personal act of singing. The tone was understated, intended to pleasantly distract passersby.

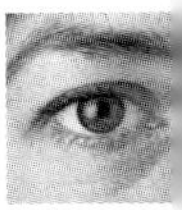

This procession of characters wound its way through crowds that jeered at them and cheered them on. Children stood in awe while parents look flustered. Like the Pied Piper, Kathy led a parade for the young at heart. She both enchanted her crowd and caused a public disturbance, creating a spectacle that provided a counterpoint to the spectacle of commerce.

—*Kathryn Walter*

Echosystem

Ecosystem: the complex of a community and its environment functioning as a unit in nature.
—New Webster's Dictionary

A small, one-watt portable radio transmitter fits into a VHS cassette case. It transmits to a radius of about a mile, depending on the antenna and other variables, and any channel can be selected by simply adjusting the main transmitter on the device itself. This inexpensive and low-tech form of sonic spatialization is what I have, since 1991, been referring to as "sonic choreography." I send a recorded soundtrack to between eight and a hundred choral performers, each of whom holds a portable radio/blaster set to the same channel. They perform live a combination of songs, text and improvisations over the recorded soundtrack. Instead of staying near microphones and behind a PA system with their trusty boomboxes, they are free to move through a space and are able to control what is essentially their own personal monitor. This allows for many more levels of audience interaction and theatricality. A great deal is left to the individual performer, who may choose to perform completely seriously or talk in between musical phrases or make up new parts. While casually strolling through the crowd, radio in hand, the performers can create an intimate atmosphere or a confrontational one. They can even entice people to sing along. Ideally, a listener can be enveloped in sound coming from several directions, like a sonic tidal wave.

Kathy Kennedy

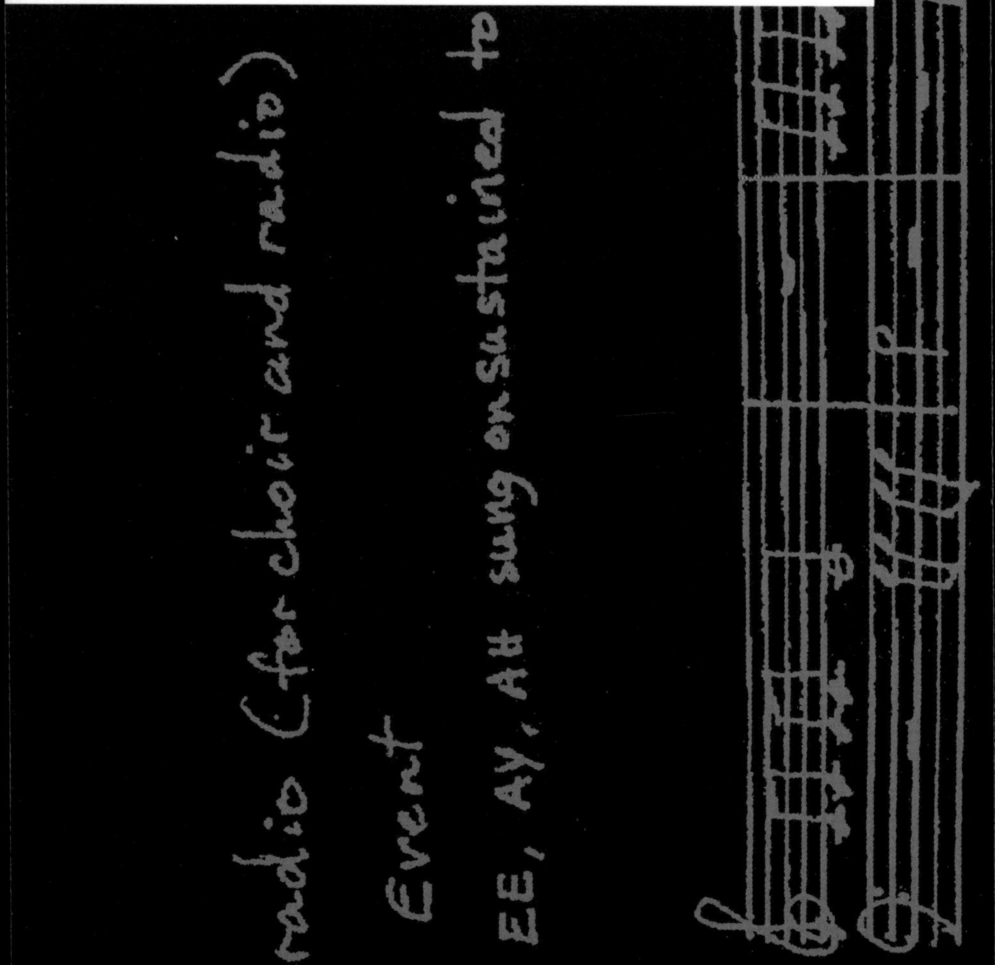

Commands ▷ ▷▷ ■, Pah-Ray-Dee-Oh, etc.
improvised by leader, live on radio transmitter.

ONE

Sustained tones, singing "one" anywhere in scale of F major.

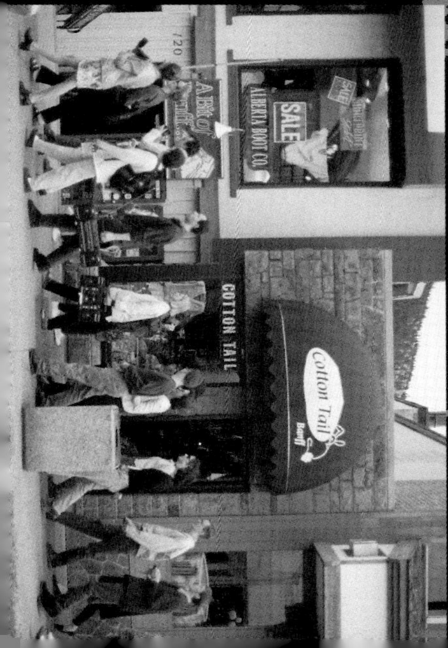

-ined exhalations, "shhh" along with sound of radio.

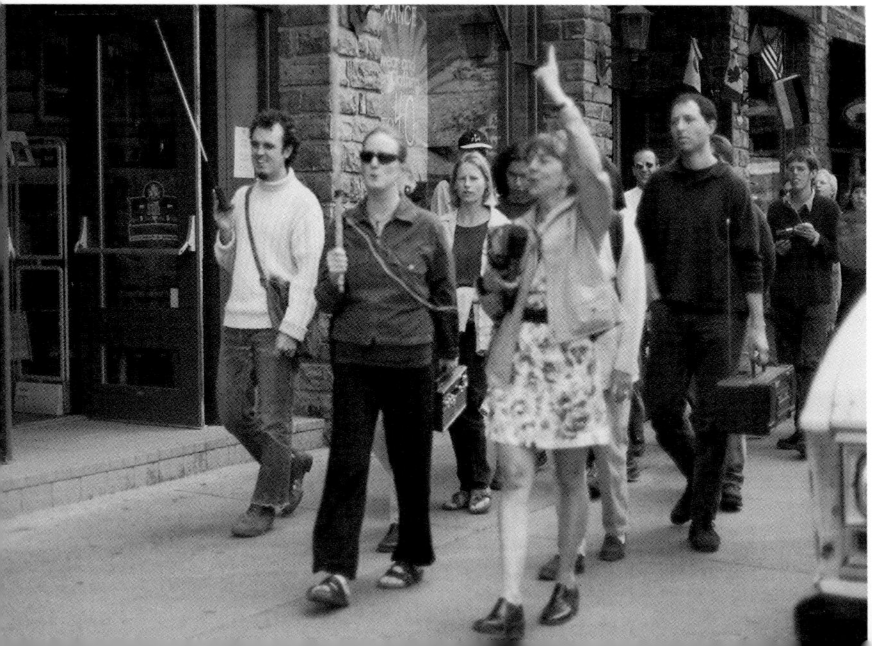

EYEWITNESS ACCOUNT

I have been witness to strange events during my stay here, but the strangest of all was Kathy Kennedy's *Paradio*—a parade with no corporate sponsor and not a veteran, a football team, a Shriner, or a Christmas elf to be seen. The location was carefully chosen: Banff Avenue is Tourism Central. People here are united by an almost manic drive to consume, and everything that passes over palms has a price tag. Kathy's performance, by contrast, worked against the currency, bucked the tourist system, drowned out the chi-ching of cash registers, obscured the cheerful signs proclaiming wares: Maple Syrup. Ice Cream. Indian Moccasins. Sushi. McDonald's. Beer.

I arrived late, and the paraders were already advancing at a snail's pace along the street, with Kathy at the head. A few people carried rigged radio receivers, set to transmit sounds like "AAAAHHHH" and "lulululululu." This was our cue to spread the sounds—"AAAAHHHH." I found myself pulled into the group, following in the tracks of someone ahead of me. One step forward, two steps back. Three jumps on the spot. Stand still. I joked to the person beside me that Kathy was our low-impact aerobics instructor, that we looked like a militia group in training with our synchronized moves and electronic transmitters.

As our sound-tunnel cut through the Saturday street traffic, a crowd began to gather. The kids dug it; the adults seemed nonplussed. I overheard one cranky woman tell her friend, "Don't worry—they'll go away soon." And later, as our chorus hit a particularly strange frequency, a man joked to his kids, "Soon only the dogs will be able to hear."

Paradio made another critical reverberation, reminding us of the role public radio has played in transmitting a rhetoric of Canadian culture from "coast to coast." Now, if only *Paradio* could replace "This Morning" as our regular morning audio-fare, maybe a new radiophonic culture could emerge—one that demonstrates greater daring, malleability, interaction and even some healthy confusion.

—*Kyo Maclear*

Windows

SCENARIO

Kathy Kennedy also created a Web site related to the theme of private investigations, making reference to cinema and issues of personal identity. This project, called *Windows*, leads the viewer, via a computer, through a number of black screens. At first these black screens reveal nothing except the viewer's own reflection—as you wait for the program to load, you are made aware of the act of looking. A sequence of flashing window images appears on the screen, creating an ambiguous architectural web. Clicking on these icons moves the viewer to other obscure sites—each window reveals a different image of the protagonist, "Kathy Kennedy" and, in fact, each window is a link to an actual or a fictitious Web site. There is a Kathy Kennedy selling real estate in Oregon, a photography dealer in New York, a math teacher in San Mateo, even family photos of one Kathy's trip to Las Vegas! Existing pages of Private Investigator Kathy Kennedy are interspersed. This mixture of found and invented identities raises questions about who is "real" in cyberspace. Which character is the true Kathy Kennedy? Can you be what you want to be in virtual space?

—*Kathryn Walter*

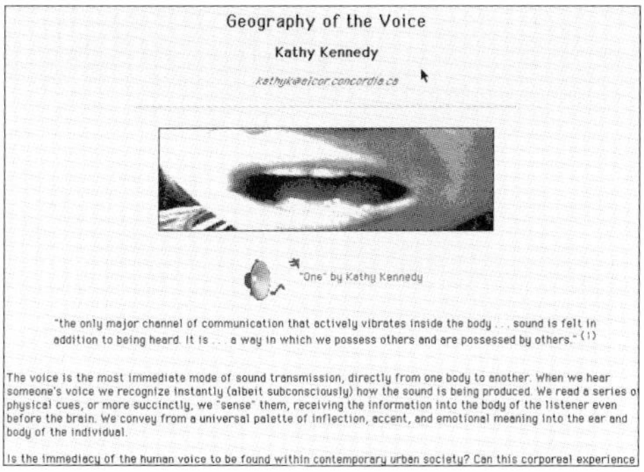
Geography of the Voice
Kathy Kennedy
kathyk@alcor.concordia.ca
"One" by Kathy Kennedy
"the only major channel of communication that actively vibrates inside the body . . . sound is felt in addition to being heard. It is . . . a way in which we possess others and are possessed by others." (1)
The voice is the most immediate mode of sound transmission, directly from one body to another. When we hear someone's voice we recognize instantly (albeit subconsciously) how the sound is being produced. We read a series of physical cues, or more succinctly, we "sense" them, receiving the information into the body of the listener even before the brain. We convey from a universal palette of inflection, accent, and emotional meaning into the ear and body of the individual.
Is the immediacy of the human voice to be found within contemporary urban society? Can this corporeal experience

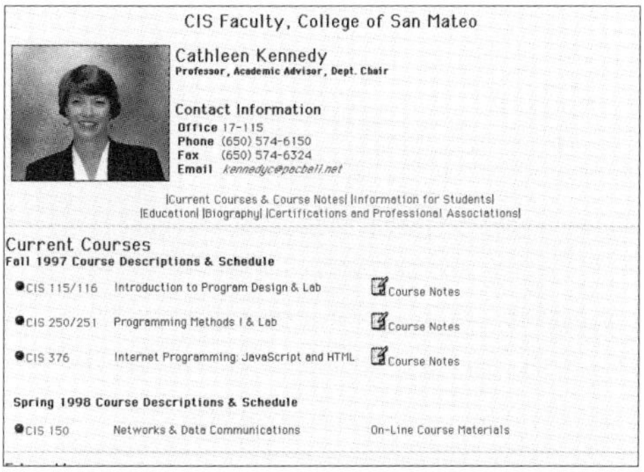
CIS Faculty, College of San Mateo
Cathleen Kennedy
Professor, Academic Advisor, Dept. Chair
Contact Information
Office 17-115
Phone (650) 574-6150
Fax (650) 574-6324
Email kennedyc@pacbell.net
|Current Courses & Course Notes| |Information for Students|
|Education| |Biography| |Certifications and Professional Associations|
Current Courses
Fall 1997 Course Descriptions & Schedule
CIS 115/116 Introduction to Program Design & Lab Course Notes
CIS 250/251 Programming Methods I & Lab Course Notes
CIS 376 Internet Programming: JavaScript and HTML Course Notes
Spring 1998 Course Descriptions & Schedule
CIS 150 Networks & Data Communications On-Line Course Materials

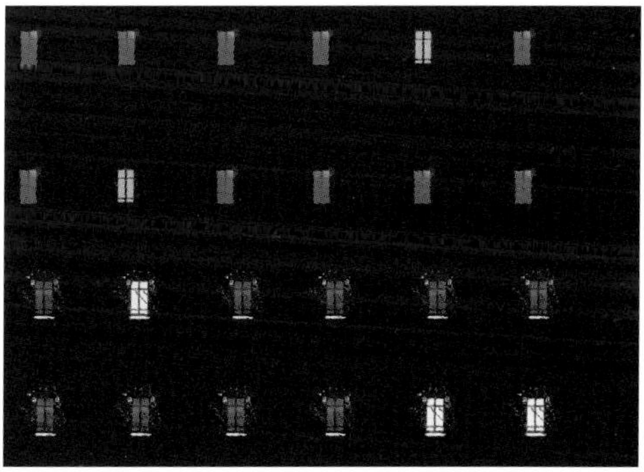

Conclusion

Kathryn Walter

Building History

In 1971, Adrian Piper walked the streets of Manhattan dressed in clothes soaked in spoiled milk. By claiming public space in such a manner, the artist made herself at once threatening and vulnerable. This piece was part of a series of artworks called *Catalysis* in which she altered her appearance as a form of intervention into public places, insinuating rupture within the status quo and contributing to a history of contemporary performance art practice. The 1970s saw many women artists use their bodies as the means for political and creative expression, and particular to this evolving tradition was an emphasis on creating personae to be assumed in the art world as well as in the streets. Other artists such as Eleanor Antin, Suzanne Lacy, Martha Wilson, Ana Mendieta, Tanya Mars and Vera Frenkel, to name only a few, were themselves both subject and object of their work, playing roles, transforming their bodies and claiming public spaces—performing transgressive acts as well as constructing situations for consciousness raising and community building.

The Private Investigators were all women in recognition of this historical trajectory of feminist cultural practice, with respect to times when inventing personae was, in fact, a political reality for women—consider artists like the Brontë sisters, George Eliot, George Sand and Colette, who used male identities to gain access to the public sphere. As women have fought for and won rights, methods of claiming and moving forward in this space have diversified in relation to social change.

Over the years, waves of feminism have broken down traditional female stereotypes and facilitated women's freedom in public places.

Though it would be too soon to suggest that the streets are entirely safe for women, contemporary artists are finding acute and sophisticated forms of political intervention that draw attention to the ironies and contradicitions integral to a society that over-determines social roles and codes of behaviour.

Before the Private Investigators made their marks, other artists and curators have also looked at Banff as a place for similar critique, and several women artists previously used this site as a critical context for performance-based work. Projects of note include Rebecca Belmore's *Ayum-ee-aawach Oomama-mowan* (1991), Jin-me Yoon's *Souvenirs of the Self* (1991), Colette Urban's *It's on your head, It's in your head* (1992), Rose English's *Princess—The Bride of an Idea* (1994), and Margo Kane's *Memories Springing, Water Singing* (1992)[1].

The Private Investigators have contributed to these local and international histories with projects as insightful as they were varied. Each artist/collaborator took a different course of action in the late-twentieth-century commercial landscape, highlighting and blurring the lines between public and private space, public and private identity and ways of seeing and being seen.

This exhibition builds on a history of cultural practices that it in turn recalls as a support system enabling projects like this to take place within established structures of public funding and institutions. Many thanks go to all who made the project enlightening, inspiring and fun.

1. The following publications discuss the works mentioned:

Between Views and Points of View, exhibition curated by Daina Augaitus and Sylvie Gilbert, catalogue of the same name produced by the Walter Phillips Gallery, 1991.

Margo Kane, *Memories Springing, Waters Singing*, one of three catalogues produced as a part of *As Public As Race*, a series of performances curated by Sylvie Gilbert, Walter Phillips Gallery, 1992.

"Urban Radio" by Tim Westbury, *Radio Rethink: Art Sound and Transmission*, ed. Daina Augaitus and Dan Lander, Walter Phillips Gallery, 1994.

Princess—the bride of the idea (exhibition flyer), a performance curated by Daina Augatis and Tim Westbury, 1994.

Biographies

Millie Chen and **Evelyn Von Michalofski** have since 1990 collaborated on several projects that investigate community as a concept and a practice. Their costume-based works examine cultural identity through the language of survival, including *Yurtopia* (Lethbridge, 1995) and *Hairbread* (Gronigen, Holland, 1993). Millie and Evelyn live in Toronto and work independently as well as collaboratively.

Shawna Dempsey and **Lorri Millan** have been collaborating full-time in a variety of media since 1989. They articulate their feminist and lesbian identity through the use of humour in their performance art, video, film and book projects. They have created a variety of characters that cleverly disrupt and challenge conventional representations of women, and their interventions in public spaces are as engaging as their stage work. Shawna and Lorri tour extensively, performing their work locally and internationally. Winnipeg is their chosen home.

Kathy Kennedy is known as a musician and sound artist, often working with the voice and new technologies. She has worked with women's communities, creating and facilitating many collaborative projects. Kathy is a principal founder of the women's digital media intervention group Studio XX and is also the founding director of the innovative women's choral group Choeur Maha, who released their first CD, *Different Angels*, in 1997. She works in Montreal and San Francisco and has participated in performances and symposia internationally.

Kyo Maclear is an independent writer and editor based in Toronto. Her first book, *Beclouded Visions: Hiroshima-Nagasaki and the Art of Witness* (State University of New York Press, 1999), addresses questions of historical memory and witnessing in twentieth-century art. Her work has been published in several art and culture magazines, including *Toronto Life*, *Brick*, *Mix*, *Fuse* and *This Magazine*.

Shelley Niro and **Faye HeavyShield** work independently. This Banff performance was their first collaboration. Shelley is well known for her photography and films that use humour to challenge Western representations of First Nations cultures. She is from the Six Nations Reserve, lives in Brantford and has exhibited her work internationally. Her latest film, *Honey Moccasin*, was released in 1998. Faye works with a variety of materials to create elegant minimalist installations that draw on personal memory. Women's clothing combined with organic fibres reflect the exchanges and conflicts between her Aboriginal and Catholic upbringing. Faye is from the Blood Reserve and currently lives in Calgary. She has exhibited her work across Canada and the U.S.

Judy Radul is an interdisciplinary artist who works in performance, video, photography and installation. She is also known for her poetry and critical writing. Her solo exhibition *Documents for Performance* (Or Gallery, Vancouver, 1998) questions the relationship between performance and document and posits both the viewer and the gallery itself as performative. Judy lives in Vancouver and has exhibited her work in Canada and abroad.

Kathryn Walter is a visual artist who uses a variety of media to consider the interface between visual art and social space. *Private Investigators* is Kathryn's curatorial debut. This project continues her research into ways that artists access, interact with and disrupt public space. She has diversified her practice to include teaching and curating, with an interest in working with others to build culture and local histories. She is currently living and working in Toronto.

Index